# THE ART AND
# LIGHT BULB MOMENTS

*Creativity is one of the mind's most mysterious processes, long thought to come and go of its own volition. But in this insightful book, Tom Evans unlocks some of the mystery and shows that this isn't the case. This is an insightful book which uncovers some of the mind's mysterious creative processes. Tom Evans shows us how we can create the right conditions which enable insight and inspiration to arise, so that don't just have to wait for them. A very practical and accessible guide to uncovering your mind's potential.*

**Steve Taylor**, Author of *Waking From Sleep, Making Time* and *Out of the Darkness*

*Tom writes beautifully and captures the magic of light bulb moments. He teaches us how to both create and ground light bulb moments and not just hope they happen. Your initial idea is just the beginning of the journey so read the book and let the adventure begin.*

**Bev James**, CEO of the James Caan Entrepreneurs Business Academy

*Tom Evans shows how everyone in a team can be encouraged to have light bulb moments which can be used throughout the entire product life cycle.*

**Mike Southon**, *Financial Times* columnist and best-selling business author

*What a wonderful tool and resource for tapping into our creative muse anytime, anyplace. Written in an accessible style this book is for anyone who wants to take an idea from inspiration to manifestation.*

**Davina MacKail**, Author of *The Dream Whisperer*

*A very nifty little book for Entrepreneurs wanting to learn how to harness the power of our ideas. It's arty, scientific and magical and much, much more useful and inspiring than Dragon's Den!*
**Judith Morgan**, Entrepreneur, www.JudithMorgan.com

*Like Tom himself,* The Art and Science of Light Bulb Moments *works powerfully and effectively on many levels; it is well-written, inspiring, practical and like a breath of fresh air for the heart and mind. If you put into practice only a fraction of the rich resources on offer in this book, you will transform your own life, and quite possibly that of many others, too. Read, digest, do - and be sure to send a copy to everyone you care about.*
**Christine Miller MA FRSA**, Founder & Editor *ReSource Magazine* & The ReSource Foundation Author: *Secret Garden of the Soul*

*Light bulb moments - we all have them but many of us do nothing about them, not least understand them. Tom's simple, easy to read book gives you a fantastic insight as to why we have them, what to do to encourage them and how to actualise them once you have them. The book is designed to either pick up and read in total (much recommended) or just cherry pick the chapters that you need to focus on at the time of reading. It gives you a roadmap to follow for your light bulb ideas. I found the ideas of sharing your light bulb moments with your team and also how they can help the solo entrepreneur progress them especially interesting. I immediately saw how outsourcing can help bridge 'The Chasm' and how you can grow your ideas at your own speed.*
**Eva Davies**, www.Outsourcing4Freedom.com

# The Art
# and Science of
# Light Bulb
# Moments

# The Art
# and Science of
# Light Bulb
# Moments

Tom Evans

BOOKS

Winchester, UK
Washington, USA

First published by O-Books, 2011
O Books is an imprint of John Hunt Publishing Ltd., The Bothy, Deershot Lodge, Park Lane, Ropley,
Hants, SO24 0BE, UK
office1@o-books.net
www.o-books.com

For distributor details and how to order please visit the 'Ordering' section on our website.

ISBN: 978 1 84694 459 8

A CIP catalogue record for this book is available from the British Library.

Design: Lee Nash

Printed in the UK by CPI Antony Rowe
Printed in the USA by Offset Paperback Mfrs, Inc

We operate a distinctive and ethical publishing philosophy in all
areas of our business, from our global network of authors to
production and worldwide distribution.

# CONTENTS

*Thanks & Acknowledgements*

To John Hunt at O Books for trusting in the concept of this book, and the team of editors and designers who helped put it on the page.

To Dave Clarke of NRG, Gerri McManus with the Scientific Medical Network, Tony Bennett, Nicky Marshall, David Nunn and Sheila Steptoe for letting me test drive the first prototypes of these ideas out at their business networking meetings.

To Judith Morgan, Janet Swift, Jackie Walker, Jenny Littlejohn, Jo Simpson ... five wonderful ladies whose names all begin with 'J' I notice. You have all been so supportive along the way and know what part you played.

Thanks to John Cassidy for the author photograph.

Thanks also to Mike Southon, Iain McGilchrist, Steve Taylor and Davina Mackail for their permission to use some of their concepts in this book.

Thanks to Chris Griffiths and his team at iMindmap for creating a true Mind Mapping software tool. The Mind Maps in this book were created using it.

Permission to use the extract (in Chapter 3) granted by Tony Buzan, the inventor of Mind Maps and Chris Griffiths - www.thinkbuzan.com

*To Louise for giving me copious amounts of Time, Space and Love*

# A Brief History of the Light Bulb Moment

Have you ever experienced a blinding flash of inspiration? Perhaps you got a whole vision for a new product, a new direction in life or even a great idea for a best selling book.

If so, congratulations, you've had a light bulb moment and experienced the Art of how to have them.

Have you ever had an idea in this way, and not done anything about it, only to see someone else bring it to market a few years later? If so, what you are perhaps missing is knowing the Science of how to capitalize on your light bulb moment.

This is what this book is all about - how to have light bulb moments on demand and then how to make them bring real world results for your benefit and for the benefit of others.

Now when we think about the light bulb, we often think of Edison who is popularized as its inventor. What is somewhat ironic is that Edison didn't really have a light bulb moment about the invention of the light bulb. If he had had a true light bulb moment, he may have come up with the scientific breakthrough that led to the energy saving bulb which, in turn, may have prevented global warming.

Edison was what is known as an empiricist. He didn't so much invent the light bulb as develop it, based on other peoples' prior work, using a process of trial and error.

One of his assistants even died in the process. He was sent on a mission in Latin America to bring back exotic bamboo samples where he contracted yellow fever and never made it back. Edison even electrocuted an elephant in the name of science, but more on why he did this later. Such is the price of scientific progress.

The electric light was first demonstrated by many people, including Humphrey Davy, 70 or so years before Edison started working on it. Davy came up with the carbon arc lamp which is still used on film sets and on ships today. What Edison actually came up with was the long lasting light bulb and his mission was to make it affordable for everyone.

"I want candles to only be affordable by the rich," he was quoted.

Edison came up with a filament that lasted about 40 hours. In order to make it work, though, he also had to develop the generating system to make it illuminate in the first place, the light switch to turn it on and off, and the Edison screw so it could be replaced at the end of its life.

It is truer to say he perfected the science of the crystallization of the light bulb moment. He actually brought the concept of the research and development laboratory to the world. He was one of the first technologists to court and extract money from venture capitalists. He continually refined, improved and cross-fertilized ideas from one field to the other. Many of the elements of the electric light system he came up with were based on his work on the telegraph and the phonograph.

He made loads of mistakes and he learned much in the process. Apocryphally, Thomas Alva Edison tried out about 10,000 or so materials for the filament before he found the one that worked best. When he was challenged on why he couldn't have scientifically worked out that one straight away, he is alleged to have said, "Yes, but now I know 9,999 things that don't work."

In turn his work naturally inspired others. His work on encoding techniques for the telegraph has led to us having incredible broadband speeds down copper wire with very limited bandwidth. Many of us now carry around a descendent of the phonograph in our pocket in the form of an MP3 player, or as one of many applications on our 'smart phones'.

Edison played this role of empiricist to his dying day. Even in his last few months, he engaged with his physicians, experimenting with diet and drugs to see what made him feel better.

Now I'm not suggesting you go as far as to challenge your

doctor or electrocute an elephant, but we will look his methods, and those of other geniuses, throughout this book so you too will learn how to bring your own ideas to life.

Scientific, artistic and even spiritual light bulb moments have occurred throughout human history.

The apostle Paul being struck by 'lightning' on the road to Damascus was probably a good example of one of them. He switched sides from being a persecutor of Christians, and others, to an evangelist.

Archimedes was set a challenge to determine the volume of an object with an irregular shape. It was a crown made for King Hiero II, who had supplied pure gold to be used to make it. The King wanted to know whether some silver had been sneaked into the mix. Archimedes obviously couldn't melt it down to a regular shape in order to work out its volume. The answer came apparently when he got in a bath and worked out, in a flash, that the volume of water displaced was proportional to density and volume of any matter.

Archimedes then took to the streets naked, so excited by his discovery that he had forgotten to get dressed, crying "Eureka!" meaning "I have found it!".

Apparently, so it turned out, some silver had indeed been mixed in; we can guess what fate befell the crown's maker.

Isaac Newton was reported to have experienced a light bulb moment when an apple fell on his head. It has been said that he got the whole of the theory of gravity in less than a second and that it took him the rest of his life to get it down on paper. The apple story paints a good image, however, it is probably an urban myth.

Leonardo da Vinci also had a light bulb moment when he came up with his drawing of the helicopter and had the prescience of caution to invent the parachute in case it didn't work.

What is interesting is that in the time of Archimedes, Da Vinci and Newton, the light bulb hadn't been invented, yet the mental faculty to experience light bulb moments has apparently been with us for many thousands of years.

Indeed they do have other names like the Archimedes' 'Eureka Moments', or the German 'Aha-Erlebnis' - or Aha Experience - coined by the psychologist Karl Bühler.

Today we call them light bulb moments and it is uncertain exactly when and where this phrase came into common usage. We all know what it means though - at the flick of a metaphorical switch, for an idea to illuminate in our heads that takes us in a new and exciting direction.

Learning how to experience them on demand is what this book is all about.

# Who is This Book for?

This book is written for inventors, scientists, teachers, businesses, students and anyone who wants to have a bright idea to change their world and indeed the world itself.

If you are a writer, musician or artist seeking a flash of inspiration for your next creation, this book is for you too.

If you are a copywriter with a deadline or want to write a sales proposal that will close the deal, there is much inspiration for you here.

It's ideal for those serial entrepreneurs who are always seeking the 'next big thing' but never seem to pull it off. This book explains why you've been experiencing frustration and what you need to do to break the old patterns that haven't worked so far.

It's written for anyone who wants to explore the true nature of thought and consciousness. I touch upon where we may be heading from an evolutionary perspective and how each one of us is an integral part of the whole process.

It's written for those that want to explore the wonderful ability we seem to possess of being self-aware.

It's written for teachers who want to show their pupils how to tap into unlimited creativity.

Equally it's written for pupils who are being taught left brained thinking who intuitively sense there must be a better way. The smart teachers will spot this and learn from their students - which of course is the best way.

It's also written for people who think misleadingly that 'thoughts become things'.

To put the record straight, thoughts don't become things, they **are** things.

If you think about it, these words are an echo of the thoughts I had when I wrote this book which in turn echo those of writers,

5

thinkers, scientists and philosophers before me.

My aim is that you will echo these in turn and allow the ripples in the pond to reach other shores.

# How to Read This Book

There are many different ways to approach this book. You can choose the one that suits you best.

Like all books, you can read it sequentially, breaking off to do the simple exercises at the end of each chapter.

Incidentally, in the first part of the book, I have called these exercises "Illuminations" as, if you could MRI scan your brain when you did them, you would see new bits of it light up. In some cases, the whole brain will illuminate when the light bulb moment arrives.

In the second part, they are called "Crystallizations" which is a critical phase in converting your light bulb moments into real world applications. This is much like a solid crystal coming out of a super-saturated liquid solution in chemistry.

You can savour this book, taking in one chapter a day so that in your sleep and dreams the learnings instill themselves into your unconscious mind and cellular neurology.

There is even a chapter on using dreams to generate light bulb moments and seeding them just before you go to sleep.

Optionally you can read the theory and explanation in a first run through of the book and come back and do the Illuminations and Crystallizations later.

You can also dive straight into a chapter that interests you, wherever it is in the book.

You may even find that just doing the illumination in chapter one gives you a light bulb moment that inspires you so much that you put the book down to work on it. You then don't have time to finish the book. If that happens to you, then I would be very happy that the book has achieved what I had intended which is to bring enlightenment and illumination to you and your world.

Why not be radical? This book is designed so it can be read

forwards or backwards, so you can start with the last chapter and end up here.

At the end of each chapter, you will find a section called Flashbacks. They encapsulate the main points of each chapter in a nutshell. They are useful for speed readers and if you want to go back over the book quickly so you can picture it as a whole in your mind's eye.

You will find resources on my web site such as links to software tools and Mind Map templates for the exercises. There are companion audio visualisations to help you enter altered and heightened states of mind. You will also find an area on my web site where you can post and discuss your light bulb moments with others.

That said, no special technology or extraordinary expense is required in order to fully immerse yourself in the world of light bulb moments. Colored pens and pencils, a reporter's note book and A3 or tabloid size paper is all you need to complete the exercises in the book. And, of course, an open mind.

There is also some recommended reading at the back of the book for those who want to research the themes I explore here in more depth.

# Part 1

# The Art

This section will take you on an experiential voyage of discovery into your own thought processes.

There is nothing new here. Indeed, much of this material is as old as the hills ... if not a little older.

The prevalent scientific wisdom is that our consciousness is an epiphenomenon - or a result of - the complexity of our brains and their billions of neurons. It is understandable why we might think that yet it doesn't by itself explain the condition of self-awareness itself.

There is a view that, if you connect enough neurons together in a certain way, our brains flip over a 'Tipping Point' and we wake up. Self-awareness after all doesn't switch on until we pass our toddling phase. As we pass through our primary school years, our sense of separateness switches on more and more as we pass into adulthood and learn and establish 'who we are'.

Now the purpose of this book is not to question or challenge conventional scientific wisdom for how consciousness arises or even to purport an opposite stance.

Rather, merely by taking a sideways view as to where our consciousness and thoughts may come from, it becomes easier to tap into light bulb moments on demand.

It is quite feasible that this is just a psychological trick of the mind caused by meditative self-reflectivity. Nevertheless these techniques seem to work and would certainly be worth further study for those with that inclination and skill. I belong to the camp where if you find something that works, don't break it or over-analyze it, just in case you spoil the magic.

So the first part of this book shows you how to become more

'art-full' in entering into a state of consciousness that stimulates, and makes you more susceptible to receive, light bulb moments.

It might be no surprise that this state is the same state of mind that artists, musicians and writers have accessed down the ages. It has many names from the contemporary 'getting in the zone' to channelling, with all its spiritual connotations.

To me, it doesn't need a necessarily need a label nor for its source to be attributed. It's a blissful state from where unlimited creativity flows.

The beauty of light bulb moments is more than the gift of a blinding flash of inspiration. When you get a true light bulb moment it is perfect in many other respects.

The timing is just exquisite. All the resources you need to make it happen seem to fall into place effortlessly. The light bulb moment seems to come along just when you need it - or the planet needs it.

The unexpected benefits seem to be numerous too. You become luckier; your business seems to improve and life on the whole becomes easier. Spin off inventions come along that you had never envisaged that are sometimes better and even more profitable than the original idea.

When you bring that first light bulb moment into physical reality, you seem to get more and more coming along.

It is almost like you are being guided.

Tapping into light bulb moments a wonderful way to be.


Enjoy.

# *I*

# What is a Light Bulb Moment?

*"If we concentrate on the content of thought, we lose the sight of its direction."*
Amit Goswami, The Self-Aware Universe

So how do you know you've had a light bulb moment as opposed to having any old thought?

The first indicator is that they seem to arrive against the 'normal' conscious stream of thought which comprises the internal dialogue and commentary we run inside our heads.

They can stop you in your tracks and make you drop everything in order to pursue them. All of a sudden, everything you have done to date seems mundane. You know you are on to the 'next big thing'.

Like our breathing and heart beat, most of us never give a second thought to our own thought processes. This is a bit of a shame as merely by thinking about our thinking and controlling our thoughts, we can modify and control the world around us at a fundamental level. It's even possible that most thoughts aren't necessarily what you think of as your own. Curious? These are themes we will explore in more depth later.

For now, just for a moment put this book down and have a think about the thoughts that are running through your mind. As you think about them, notice that the first thought you had seems to get replaced by the second and the third and so on.

This might sound simplistic or even a bit weird if you've never thought about this before. Notice even as you even think about what I have written and you are now reading how any other thoughts seem to get pushed to one side.

The upshot is that when we are engaged in what we think of as 'conscious thought', this is enough to block any other thoughts from coming in.

This phenomenon has attracted the rather fancy sounding name of the Quantum Collapse of Thought and there is an audio visualization that accompanies this book to help you experience this state more deeply. This process, by the way, is similar to 'counting sheep' to get to sleep.

Light bulb moments tend to come in when you are least expecting them and they also seem to appear in less than a second. It's almost like you have jumped out of time. The reason for this is that's sort of what has happened.

Like Newton when he was apocryphally hit on his head by that apple, you get the whole vision - and sounds, smells and tastes - in what appears to be no time at all.

Very strong light bulb moments also seem to hit every cell of your body. Your heart can beat faster; you get excited and just can't wait to get all the ideas down on paper before they disappear from your memory.

You get a really good 'gut feeling' about it. Incidentally, we will explore in this book how phrases like 'gut feeling' in common usage in our language give much away as to what is actually going on. When we say things like "Off the top of my head", that's a good clue as to where the associated thought actually comes from.

So light bulb moments seem to occur outside your 'normal' stream of consciousness. You may get one when driving home from work, while ironing, when painting or mowing the lawn. The common factor here is that you are doing something else entirely other than trying to come up with an idea for the 'latest, greatest thing'.

They don't tend to happen when you are immersed in something like a film or a concert. Here the external experience kind of takes over your consciousness.

Light bulb moments also have a tendency to be repeated if you ignore them. You may see an example that reminds you of your idea in a newspaper or on TV. Perhaps someone says something at a dinner party that reminds you of your vision. You may even have a vivid dream about it. The repetition is often in a different, or slightly modified form, so that you notice it and pay attention to it.

As we will explore, some light bulb moments do indeed come in your dreams or you may be even awakened with one. Between 2am and 4am in the morning is a common time for this to happen. You are then are kept awake thinking about them, unable to get back to sleep or you may even be driven to awaken fully and write the ideas down.

Light bulb moments that occur in dreams can often come in an allegorical or metaphorical form. For example, the German organic chemist Kekulé was trying to work out the molecular structure for benzene which he knew had six carbon and six hydrogen atoms. He had a dream about a snake biting its tail and subsequently discovered, or uncovered, the benzene ring which became the basis for all organic chemistry.

So the key to having a light bulb moment is not to try too hard to have one and your mind may come up with it anyway.

If you screw your face up and try and think of something, that word that's on the tip of your tongue, it won't come in. Perhaps you have known that you knew the answer to a quiz question or the name of someone you met in the street by accident. Frustratingly at the time, the answer or name eludes you but you remember it sometime later, again when not thinking about it.

Edison however didn't relax and just let the idea for the right filament material come in naturally. He took the sledgehammer approach and tried everything known to man (and woman) until he found something that worked.

There is nothing wrong with this technique per se and, as I

mentioned, he did find out lots about what didn't work too. This all adds to the collective thought pool.

As you will see though, there is a much smarter way to go about the whole process of invention and that's to think about something else entirely but on purpose rather than by chance.

As mentioned, at the end of each chapter, there is a simple example which demonstrates the principles we explore. You can either complete it now or move on to the next chapter and come back and do it later.

## Illumination 1: Disassociation

I am sure you are familiar with the process of word association. I say "dog", you say "cat", the next person might say "caterpillar", the next "tank" and so on. So within just a few steps, we've got from a warm mammal, to an insect larva, to a killing machine. All without consciously having to think about it.

The fact that our brains can do this within the blink of an eye in itself is incredible. Even the fastest computer cannot currently make these lateral associations and each pairing or grouping of people will come up with amazingly different outcomes. This infinity of permutations is what spawns invention and innovation and this exercise is designed to demonstrate that ability in us.

As I mentioned, be prepared and be warned that you may not read the rest of this book. I do this exercise in my workshops and often people are taken off in amazing new directions as a result.

Just in case you don't get to read chapter 2, this exercise is also equally good for either coming up with new ideas or getting unblocked.

Its power is belied by its simplicity.

Step 1: Go and get any book (you can use this one) and make a note of how many pages it contains.

Step 2: Get a sheet of paper - as large as possible - A3 or tabloid.

Step 3: In the centre, draw a circle or a cloud and, inside it, a picture of what it is you would like to explore - an opportunity or a problem.

Step 4: Draw four branches or lines out from the central image but only going half way to the edge of the page (ie. leave some room).

Step 5: Think of any number between say 10 and the total number of pages in the book. Open the book at that page number and think of another number between 1 and 10. Count down that number of lines and find the first noun (or word that appeals to you) on that line. Write that word on one of the four branches.

Step 6: Repeat step 5 three times for each of the other main branches.

Step 7: Do this rapidly and without thinking about it. On new branches from each of the four main branches, write down 3 or 4 words that the come to mind from the main branch word in relation to the central image. If more words again come to mind, add these as third level branches.

Step 8: Relax ... and see if the process has given you a new perspective or idea.

Once completed, you should have ended up with something looking like the example image overleaf. You may also have seen a new aspect of the subject that you were 'thinking' about.

You can also combine any of the first, second and third level branch words to form new seeds or even light bulb moments.

What you can then do is take this phrase and use it as the central theme and repeat the process with a new set of words. I guarantee you will experience a new insight and perspective on the initial opportunity or problem.

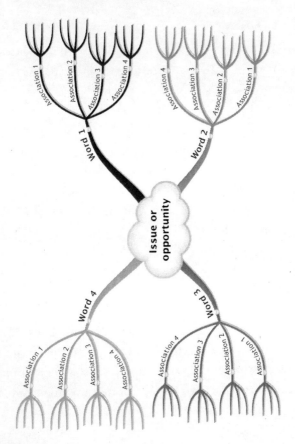

## Flashbacks

Light bulb moments come in when you least expect them.
They occur in less than a second.
They represent a disassociation in your thought stream.
They can be repeated in different forms if you ignore them or
    don't at first spot them.

# 2

# What Stops Light Bulb Moments?

*"Genius is one percent inspiration and ninety nine percent perspiration."*
Thomas Alva Edison

Before we explore the states of mind and consciousness that are ideal for experiencing light bulb moments on demand, it's worth exploring what stops them coming in.

For example, have you ever experienced road rage?

Your blood would have been boiling at the effrontery of some one cutting in front of you. They may have innocently just stolen what you felt was your bit of road space or, worse still, endangered your life and that of your family. You feel aggrieved and incensed and you may even be seeking revenge.

I think you'll agree this is hardly a time to have a light bulb moment.

Similarly, if you are going for your annual employment review or about to do a presentation, you may be rehearsing what you are about to say in your head. This too is enough to stop any external blinding flash of inspiration from coming in.

Try not-thinking about it instead, and you may be rewarded by a gem of insight that will make all the difference to your presentation.

How many times have you replayed a conversation you wished had gone differently? This internal dialog we play inside our heads, which no-one else can hear, also blocks the very source of ideas.

Imagine in that incident where you experienced road rage, if your thought stream switched from out and out revenge and anger to thinking about what caused your aggressor to behave in such a way.

Perhaps they had just been cut up by someone else moments before, or even unknowingly by you. Perhaps they were ill or had earlier argued with someone at home or at work or indeed while driving on their mobile cell phone.

Perhaps the road layout was less than ideal and a letter from you to the local council to point this out might save a life. You could take your road rage as a turning point and decide that commuting is not for you. The incident may even inspire you write a novel called Road Rage.

The point being that by disassociating from the state of anger, as per the exercise in the last chapter, you end up going down a different road which might even have a beneficial outcome.

The alternative might be you ending up at your destination, being angry all day and even taking your anger out on someone else.

The great inventors throughout history have taken an existing situation or predicament, seen it as an opportunity and then they've done something about it.

Your response to that road rage incident is a pattern which in psychological terms is known as a gestalt. Gestalts are repetitive and learned algorithms built up in our neurology to help us respond to certain situations. They are imprinted on us throughout our lives and we even pick up some from our mother's emotional state while we are in the womb. It's thought that some are imprinted on the very the RNA and DNA that we are born with.

Road rage, for example, comes from our instinct for self-preservation or 'fight or flight' response. Fight would kick off the instinct for revenge. Flight would cause you to back off. As humans though, we are fortunate to possess a self-awareness that could instigate a third way which is to reflect on the incident itself, how it made us feel and what we can do about it.

Road rage is an example of just one of several raw emotions that are enough to block light bulb moments.

Another is sadness. If you are grieving or mourning the loss of anything, from a person or pet who has passed away to a five dollar bet at the races, the imposed self-reflectivity or regret acts as a block.

If you are feeling guilty about something, this again leads to an inner dialog that can replay endlessly inside your head, blotting out all other thought processes. Externally the only sign that this might be happening is that your eyes are either closed or lowered and pointing downwards to the left.

If you are hurting, either physically or mentally, the light bulb moments won't flow. Pain anywhere on the body, especially the head, is the bane of creativity.

Fears also have a huge influence on the creative process. They can also kick in and have the most destructive influence after light bulb moments have occurred.

I first came across this in my work with authors in clearing writer's block and I have experienced them all myself to varying degrees.

The four common fears that will block the grounding of a light bulb moment are:

- the fear of failure
- the fear of ridicule
- the fear of the unknown
- the fear of success

These fears are other examples of gestalts. We need to be careful not to imprint these on our children. They are especially impressionable up the age of seven before their conscious mind has gained self-awareness and developed a degree of discrimination. As the ego forms, between the ages of 7 and 14, we are shown the child before they become the adult, much as the splendor of the butterfly as it emerges from the chrysalis.

So if you were told at school your writing was terrible, or someone laughed at a poem you wrote, that's enough to stop you being an author for a life time. Some people figure the best way to avoid failing or being ridiculed is not to put your head above the parapet. If you don't try, you can't possibly fail.

Another great self-protection strategy is to keep everything just as it is and to steer well clear of the unknown or unfamiliar. A new invention could well rock the boat so it's best not to pursue it. The unknowns will always remain unknown to you. This is bliss in many peoples' world.

Success too might not be all it's cracked up to be. You could set yourself up for a fall or get stressed about the responsibility it brings.

"Best to keep a low profile," you may hear yourself saying.

Harbouring such fears stops the pursuance of the light bulb moment dead in its tracks.

If Edison had plenty of inner demons and a fair share of external detractors and distractions, and if he had paid heed to these, we may not have had the light bulb itself and I might not be writing this book, with this title at least.

Once we learn to appreciate what stops us, simply noticing or detecting potential destructive patterns of being, doing and thinking, can be enough to increase our creativity several-fold.

As you adopt a new way of thinking, new neural pathways are established in your brain and indeed your brain chemistry even changes its composition. This has the result that you become better and better at having ideas "off the top of your head". When you then add the techniques you will learn in the later in this book on top of this, you will become unstoppable.

There is one additional caveat though which can be enough in itself to hold you back. Once you learn how to generate light bulb moments on demand, you can easily generate a glut of them. This can result in an overload and not knowing which idea to proceed with first.

Again, this is something we will deal with in the second part of the book through a filtering process which brings the best ideas to the top of the pile.

## Illumination 2: Clearing the Air

Most of the emotional states describe above can be improved by talking therapies or therapeutic techniques such hypnosis, regression, meditation and the very effective Emotional Freedom Technique.

Alternatively just going for a good walk can do the trick.

Another common method is just to get things off your chest and clear the air.

On a large piece of paper, draw a central image that represents your overall state of mind right now - or what's on it.

Then, just as you did for the last illumination, draw four branches from the centre, leaving space to append sub-branches to them as shown on the image overleaf.

Starting top right and moving clockwise, on the first, label it "What are you afraid of?" and on sub-branches list a few things that you most fear.

On the second, label it "What annoys you?" and on sub-branches list a few things that irritate you the most.

On the third, label it "What's stopping you?" and on sub-branches, in the context of innovation, list the things that prevent you from moving forward.

On the third, label it "Who stops you?" and on sub-branches, list people who currently stand in your way or get in your way.

At the end, you will either feel relieved at doing this or be inspired to do something about one or more of your current irritations.

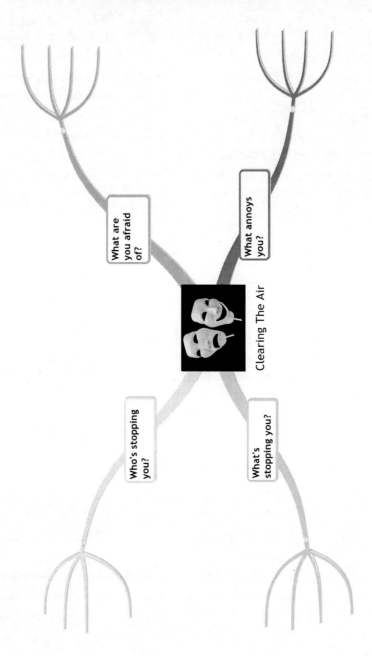

## Flashbacks

If you are actively thinking, light bulb moments won't arrive.
They are blocked by extreme emotions.
If you harbour fears, they act as a barrier to success.
If you are faced with adversity, this can trigger them so long
   as you adopt a positive frame of mind.

*3*

# Maps in Your Mind

*"The human brain does not think in toolbars and menu lists. It thinks organically like all natural forms. To think well it needs a tool that reflects that organic flow. The Mind Map is that tool."*
Tony Buzan and Chris Griffiths, Mind Mapping for Business

If you have ever been on an underground or subway system, without even thinking about it consciously, you navigated your way around using a map.

If you were familiar with the subway, you would have been carrying the parts of the map that you needed in your head. If you are like me, this would even include details like which carriage to get on so you had to walk the least distance to the exit or interchange when you got off.

For an unfamiliar subway, you might carry a physical map or refer to one on the train or platform. What you may not have appreciated about this map is that is doesn't necessarily corre-spond to the actual layout of the tracks underground. That said, the color coding and equi-distant spacing of stations makes it easy to grasp.

The London Underground map we use today was created by Henry Beck back in 1933 and has been copied by subway and overground systems around the world, such is its usefulness.

So, for example, imagine you had never been to Tokyo but I gave you a map with both Narita Airport and Akiabara circled. If I told that Narita is where you will fly into and Akiabara is where to buy the cheapest electronic goods, I reckon you could easily make your way there and pick up a bargain - all without knowing a word of Japanese.

Such maps though, only have limited usefulness as they are only metaphors. If you are in London and want to go from Waterloo Station to Covent Garden using the Underground, you might take the Northern Line to Leicester Square and the Piccadilly Line to Covent Garden. Apart from this costing you some money, and necessitating a crowded journey underground, it's actually as quick to walk across the footbridge, take in a great view of London and be a little fitter into the bargain, and on a sunny day, it's a lot more pleasant too.

We store maps in our minds for more than just navigation around the world. I have a map in my mind of where the keys on the keyboard are as I am typing these words.

I have another map for how to take my thoughts on light bulb moments and string them together in what I hope are logical and easy to follow steps.

We have maps for how to tie a shoelace, how to make spaghetti bolognese, how to drive a car, and how to light a fire. If we don't know how to do any of these things, we have another map that tells us where to find the information or how to watch someone else do it and copy them.

If all else fails, we have another map and a strategy with which we may look up a tradesman and call them up for professional help, or ask someone who knows how to help us or show us how do it .

The map to mimic and copy others is something we are born with. This map is in the very fabric of our cells. Our cells in turn have maps that allow them to replicate and become neurons, blood, organs, skin, bones and muscles. These groupings of cells then store maps for how to unconsciously breathe, regulate blood sugar and to keep our heart beating.

En masse and in concert, they also give us the ability to think and be self aware.

You can also see these maps disappearing in people who are suffering from dementia. They might not recognize a family member or fail to know what day of the week it is. Their internal sat-nav has become corrupted

Maps are also embedded into the very fabric of space, time and inorganic matter. The mass and behaviors of sub-atomic particles act as maps from which complex molecular structures form and either remain stable, decay or react.

This is the 'stuff' we are made from. The most complex molecule we know about, **DNA,** even contains the map to replicate itself and to create life. Single celled amoebae have a map of how to replicate. Plants contain a map to tell them their roots should go down into the earth and their leaves should point at and follow the Sun. Spiders are pre-programmed to weave intricate and functional webs.

Animals such as parrots, cats, dogs and horses can be taught to replicate complex routines and even invent new ones themselves.

Whales and dolphins navigate using their own natural global positioning system using a combination of ocean currents, salinity, temperature and magnetism as their guide. Birds also use the magnetic flux of the Earth, and some experts think they even use the stars, to help them literally come home to roost after migrations of thousands of miles.

Such repetition over many generations, along with the new learnings and discoveries, also gets embedded in that same DNA that creates life in the first place. Thus the whole circle of life completes, self-replicates and extends itself.

You can see an example of this in microcosm. My generation born in the 1950s and 1960s found it easier than our parents to pick up driving, computers and using remote controls. The current generation leaves many of their parents cold with their seeming ability to multi-task and incredible speed on a computer keyboard or texting a message on their phone.

The maps with which we navigate our way through life and around our physical world are embedded in neural pathways. Some pathways and patterns can be destructive like the gestalts mentioned in the last chapter. A glass half empty pathway will tend to pessimistic outcomes and a glass half full mentality will lead to invention and creativity. Just imagine what a glass overflowing mentality would be like.

Without perhaps appreciating it, in the Illuminations in the last two chapters you were drawing Mind Maps.

As you will see, Mind Maps are one of the best tools ever invented for creativity, learning and memory retention.

They are the brain-child of Tony Buzan - quiet literally the progeny that came from his brain. Incidentally, intentional use of hyphenation to concatenate and fragment words and phrases, like brain-child, is something that is really useful for illumination and illustration.

While there are many great software tools available on the market, the best way to be truly creative with Mind Maps is to hand draw them. At least, that is, until the creation of the map is second nature and embedded such that using a computer doesn't interfere with your creative flow.

On my creative writing workshops, computers are banned, even though I am a technophile.

The reason Mind Maps work so well is that they mirror the way the brain operates. The brain 'thinks' radially and by association. So say we want to invent something that is quicker, smarter, faster and cheaper. We don't start from scratch, we take an example of what works already, then we study its limitations and improve on it.

Where light bulb moments come into the equation is when a giant leap is made. Perhaps taking one solution and applying it to great effect in a completely different field. Velcro, Teflon and even the now ubiquitous text message are examples of this.

Text messaging, for example, was invented as a way for engineers to communicate with each other when debugging the early mobile phone networks. It has now grown into one of the most used services and biggest revenue generators for mobile phone operators.

So the light bulb moment doesn't just come from linear extrap-
olation but as a step change from seeing new applications which
come along from new associations.

The light bulb moment comes from that amazing near-instan-
taneous feat performed by our brains, that of pattern recognition.
We store patterns of images, sounds, smells, tastes and touch. A
whiff of a few molecules of carbolic soap is all that is needed to
take me back to primary school which, in turn, might conjure up
a memory of a teacher, a school bully or a cast iron radiator.
These three are in no way connected, by the way.

The strength of the light bulb moment has a correlation to the
number of neurons that actually 'light up'. This has been seen on
functional MRI scans.

As our brains are physical forms made of much of the same
stuff as our muscles, it may come as no surprise that they
perform better when exercised and fed regularly.

Our brains constitute only 5% off our body mass yet they
consume 20% to 25% of our energy. They take nutrients from our
blood which in turn is primarily fed from oxygen.

So it will come as no surprise therefore that correct breathing
is something that affects our brain power and we will explore
that later. We also tend to ignore the fact that the chemistry of our
bodies affects our thought processes. Being intoxicated or under
the influence of drugs is a prime example of this. The food we eat
also affects our mental performance as does the state of mind that
we are in when preparing and consuming it.

Indeed predisposition is vitally important in this regard. A
drunkard may literally stare at a glass half empty whereas a wine
connoisseur will see the smallest amount of liquid in a glass as
nectar. The way we think is wrapped up in its own circle with our
body chemistry. If we have positive thoughts, we will think
positively and we will largely experience positive outcomes.

In the same way, if you follow the steps in this book, you

cannot fail but to have light bulb moments. This will affect others around you.

My intent is to show you how to enjoy unlimited creativity. Hopefully this will rub off on you and you will in turn spread this to others.

It will come as no surprise that I have not made all of this up from scratch. I have taken some exoteric (ie. known stuff), mixed it with some esoteric teachings (ie. largely unknown) and made 1+1=3 or even more.

So now you appreciate the value of a good map, the remainder of this book is devoted to giving you a navigation system to tap into light bulb moments on demand.

This is why Mind Mapping is a great starting point from which to operate, where many light bulb moments will occur.

To get the best results from Mind Mapping, it's best to follow some simple rules.

Firstly, as you have seen, it's best to use an image to depict the central theme of the map. If you don't have one in mind, then a stylish question mark, an image of a light bulb or a smiley face will do for the purposes of this book. The image acts as a seed for the mind to start its journey of association. As such choosing one that puts you in a positive frame of mind is beneficial.

The map spreads from the central image in radial branches which are ideally of different colors. These branches act as place-holders for words or more images still.

The colors can also convey meanings. For example, green for growth or red for danger, or pink for a loving thought. The true power of the map lies in these semantics and metaphors, as it is these that stimulate the unconscious mind to bring ideas to our conscious awareness. We are also better able to remember the map in this form.

When placing words on the branches, it's advisable to use one word per branch as it makes free association easier, as per the diagram below where I mapped out associations that came to me from the phrase 'light bulb moment'.

Note too how the shape and direction of the line can also convey meaning. Like the downward, black spiral of depression. If I had used the complete phrase "light bulb moment" as the

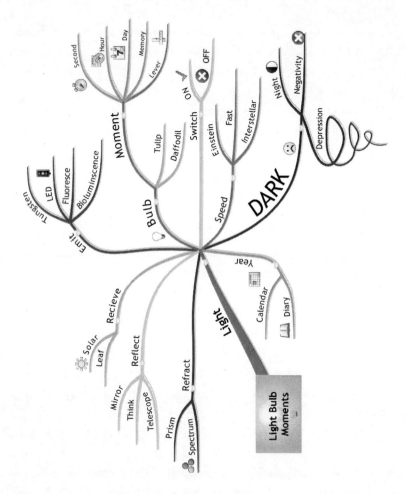

seed for my map, it would have restricted where my mind could go. From this diagram, you can see how I can generate ideas for chapters of a book or spin off ideas.

For example, recalling that light splits into a spectrum made me wonder if light bulb moments themselves had different 'colors' or 'flavors'. This was something I hadn't fully considered until I did this map. It spawned a new train of thought that in turn led to at least one whole new chapter in this book - and a sequel. Such is the power of a good map.

**Illumination 3: Your Life Journey**
So, before you set off into an amazing future full of inspirational moments, it's worth looking back on your life so far.

It may surprise you that you've almost certainly experienced many light bulb moments in your life already. They are a natural phenomenon which we can choose to embrace or ignore. This is the benefit of having free will.

So taking another piece of paper, draw an image in the centre that represents the essence of you.

For the branches this time, you can have a bit more creative control and feel free to draw sub branches with as many levels as you like.

Bear in mind the basic guidelines below to making this Life Map which you will find helpful.

- use color
- use images on sub branches if you like
- where possible, use one word per branch or an image

What you want to capture in this map is all the highlights of your life so far. Examples include:

- successes
- changes in direction
- happy coincidences
- loves
- family, friends, pets
- career, job, business
- academic, artistic and sporting achievements

Purposely I have not included an example of this map as an image as I don't want you to be influenced in any way.

## Flashbacks

We navigate our way around our complex world using maps. Our very existence is built on a map.

Mind Maps are the most useful tool you will come across to foster light bulb moments.

Having some sort of map is useful for most journeys.

# 4

# The Devil on Your Shoulder

*"It turns out that the Emissary has his own will, and secretly believes himself to be superior to the Master. And he has the means to betray him."*
The Master and his Emissary - Iain McGilchrist

The functions of our left and right brains are pretty much entrenched in popular psychology. In many a Tom & Jerry cartoon you see a devil appearing on one shoulder and an angel on the other. You may not have noticed but it is common urban mythology for the devil to be on the left shoulder and the angel on the right shoulder.

If you get a great idea, the devil might whisper things like, "Don't be silly, it will never work" and "Isn't this just like every other invention you've come up with?"

We are brought up with seemingly intrinsic knowledge that left brained thinkers are logical and even cold and calculating. Yet the right brained amongst us who are creative and intuitive are almost dismissed as dreamers having their heads in the clouds. Clearly this division and rough functional classification for the brain hemispheres isn't fruitful and reeks of a 'glass half full' mentality.

Great art, music and literature have been produced by right brained artists, musicians, and writers. It is thought that all those amazing scientific advances and leaps of understanding of our physical world have been made by those left brained thinkers.

In actual fact, it is a safe bet that all significant works of art, discoveries and inventions came into being when the progenitor was using both hemispheres in harmony. This is a mode referred to as Whole Brain Thinking.

More specifically, if your 'thinking' is biased to one side or the other, it has the tendency to block light bulb moments and their subsequent development.

The brain is just not so simple a structure for such a broad classification to be applied. The human brain contains about the same number of neurons as the stars in our galaxy - about 100 billion.

This statistic in itself triggered a light bulb moment in me that it's too coincidental not to deserve some further study.

Much of the understanding of our brain's functions comes from the study of damaged brains or the mentally ill. There are numerous research papers on the performance and capabilities of people suffering from strokes, psychosis, accidental trauma or degenerative diseases.

As a result, neurologists have a pretty good idea of what most regions of the brain process in terms based on all types of external sensory stimuli we receive through our senses. They can also see from magnetic resonance imaging which areas run the subsequent 'thought processes'. Then based on these 'thoughts' it can be deduced which other areas of the brain control our bodily movement and vocal chords.

At the same time, our unconscious mind regulates our biochemistry to keep us alive without our conscious awareness. We also have a good idea which parts of the brain are involved in these processes.

The Mind Map opposite shows the conventional model of how our brains interact with our environment and our bodies.

In this simplistic model, everything we do is predicated on an external stimulus. There is no space for random, unrequited thought to appear, as might happen in meditation, while having a shower or when you are out for a walk – these being typical of the types of conditions from where light bulb moments appear.

Based on one of these random thoughts, you might want to go

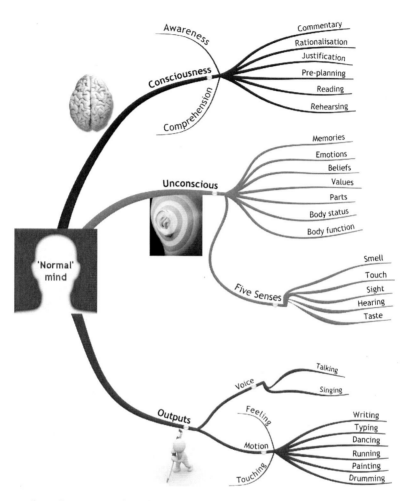

and make a cup of coffee or write a musical masterpiece. All on the whim of a thought.

In Iain McGilchrist's excellent book, The Master and His Emissary, he gives an incredibly detailed account of how the two halves of our brain interact, intercommunicate and indeed suppress each other so that the other can better function in differently appropriate situations.

He cites the function of a chicken's brain where the right eye is looking for individual grains to eat on the ground (processed by the left brain). Meanwhile at the same time, the right brain (fed by the left eye) is scanning for predators.

Note that neuroscientists can now anesthetise (or switch off) one of our hemispheres (or individual regions) temporarily to see how we then perform.

For you reading this book, for example, your left brain will be processing individual words while simultaneously the right brain works out the overall context. If anything you read makes you stop and think, or confuses you, what happens is that both hemispheres have a little debate and discussion. It is remarkable that all of this can happen without us giving it a second thought.

Note that there is a lot of intercommunication between the front and back of each hemisphere too. What is also of interest and note is that the relative use of our left and right hemispheres has changed over our history and varies in different societies. Much of this bias gets programmed in through our education and culture. For example, it has been shown that where language is depicted in pictograms, a right brain bias is detectable.

The right brain also tends to process new information and when it is learnt and ingrained, it gets passed to the left hemisphere of the brain to process. Driving a car or typing on a keyboard being two classic examples. Try driving on the other side of the road or using a keyboard with a different layout and you will get thrust back into that right brained mode of learning.

Our education system, which tends to favour learning by rote, repetition and example, biases us to a left brained existence. Especially if, as happened to me when I was 13, you were forced to choose between studying science or art and music. I've made some amends since.

In the context of experiencing light bulb moments, it is vital that both hemispheres are working in concert. Over the course of processing the idea, the different hemispheres will take on their respective roles. For example, when working on the detail of your invention, the left side may be dominant. When brainstorming all the possible spin offs, the right side may take precedence.

You can imagine the internal dialog between the hemispheres when you are Mind Mapping.

The left brain says to the right brain, "Aha, a map! I do the map reading around here, leave this to me."

The right brain, seeing that the left brain is busying itself in the detail says, "Great, now I can be truly creative."

The same type of dialog occurs when we are painting or writing - especially when we're typing on a computer or using a mouse or tablet.

So most of our days are spent flipping from one hemisphere to another. It used to be thought that the structure called the corpus callosum mainly passed information between both sides of the brain. Current wisdom is that it actually suppresses one side while the other carries out a task.

To foster the generation of light bulb moments on demand, the suppression mechanism itself has to be suppressed. When you do this, your brain truly lights up.

You then enter a state of Whole Brain and indeed Whole Mind Thinking permanently which in turn leads to a new way of being.

## Illumination 4: Walking and Cross Crawling

Each neuron in our brain needs a blood supply to bring it nutrients. Otherwise, it will either die or, at the very least, become dormant and atrophy. This can happen as we age.

A simple and effective way to keep our brain active is to exercise. This doesn't mean a strenuous workout at a gym. Just walking for 20 to 30 minutes a day is enough and, if you can, at a pace that gets you just short of being breathless.

Walking not only increases heart rate but blood flows to parts of your body and brain that it doesn't normally reach. I often go for a walk with clients and it is amazing how a good walk frees up the most stubborn mental blocks.

What walking also does is move the cerebrospinal fluid

around that our brains float in. This fluid incidentally, and almost literally, takes the weight off our minds using the principle Archimedes uncovered all those years ago.

A specific type of walking seems to move it around even more, and increases the connection and communication between right and left hemispheres.

This exercise is in two parts which can be done separately, or combined if you feel particularly energetic. It seems appropriate linguistically to call them steps.

Step 1: Walking
If you are able, go for a 20 to 30 minute walk each day.

For at least five minutes of the walk, swing your arms from side to side in front of your body. Depending on where you are or your physical ability, this movement can be as small or large as you feel comfortable with.

Step 2: Cross crawling
You can do this exercise in the comfort of your own home and it important that you do it slowly.
1. Stand with your arms to the side and let the tension fall from your body. Feel the floor with your feet.
2. Now bend your right leg at the knee and swing your left arm in front of you across your navel and touch your left elbow to your right knee. Or as close as you can manage at this stage.
3. Let your right leg fall gently and your left arm return and now bend your left leg at the knee and touch your right elbow to the left knee. Again make sure your left arm crosses your navel.
4. Try to repeat the exercise 15 to 20 times for each side.
If you find it difficult or you seem to get your sides mixed up (like tapping your head and rubbing your stomach at the same time), don't worry. This just means your left and right

hemispheres really need this exercise. Either really slow the movements down or try it lying down. It will come in time.

Also, if you suffer from back pain or are otherwise infirm, just reaching for or touching your knee with the fingers of the opposite hand will be sufficient to induce the effect.

I first did this exercise over 10 years ago and after the exercise I briefly started mirror writing. This is often a trait seen in those categorised with dyslexia. If it happens to you, take it as a sign that new pathways are opening up in your brain. Incidentally, the exercises in the next chapter are perfect for those who feel any dyslexic tendencies are blocking them from being creative.

Note if you are physically infirm or unwell and either of these exercises is either impossible or likely to cause you harm, consult with your doctor or medical advisor before undertaking them.

If you cannot do either exercise, you can actually get some benefit by closing your eyes and imagining you are carrying them out.

Such is the power of the mind.

## Flashbacks

Asymmetric thinking is worse than using just half your brain power.

Whole Brain Thinking is better than the two halves summed together.

Our mainstream educational system and culture is currently biased to left brain thinking.

You can use a simple exercise to correct any imbalance.

## 5

# Re-minding Yourself

*"This we know. Man did not weave the web of life; he is merely a strand in it. Whatever he does to the web, he does to himself. Whatever befalls the earth befalls the sons and daughters of the earth. All things are connected. This we know."*
Chief Seattle

Much of our modern world has come about as a direct result of the amazing analytical capabilities of our left brains. The left brain's attention to detail is mediated by the right brain's ability to hold the complete vision.

Sometimes these abilities and strengths lie in different people in a team. The mad inventor with a glut of ideas and no practicality is an example of this stereotype. The non-risk taking accountant or lawyer being their natural counterpart.

The seemingly inexorable progress that modern humankind has followed fits into a repeatable and recognizable process. First we learn or experience something new; we then make new associations; then we find new applications.

Even when an amazing new invention appears seemingly 'out of the blue', it is always possible to find an audit trail of prior art upon which it was based.

As I mentioned, the modern day iPod and MP3 player would not have come about if it wasn't for Edison's phonograph. Similarly, Charles Babbage's Difference Engine was the prototype for most modern day micro-processors.

In time, I am sure, we may have 'pods' directly implanted in our brains allowing us to communicate with the outside world and 'file share' upon the whim of a thought. Connecting between such 'pods' would give us a form of telepathy. Such a development would of course be beset with ethical implications. However, by investigating where ideas come from, this particular development may prove to be completely unnecessary in the first place.

Any innovation, like telepathic brain implants, starts in our own imagination, often first appearing in fiction or science fiction only to come into being a few years later. This time frame too seems to be reducing. The gap between HG Wells' book 'The First Men in the Moon' (1901) to the actual Moon landings was 70 years. Our mobile phones are effectively the Communicator carried about by Captain Kirk and Mr Spock in Star Trek in the Sixties. This is a gap of only 30 years. There are innumerable other examples.

By generating light bulb moments on demand and bringing them into physical reality, this gap can be shortened even further. At the same time, our ability to intercommunicate with each other increases.

We have to take a journey back in time to see how.

It's been observed that indigenous tribes' people don't have the same sense of separateness from each other and nature that we experience. They are in tune with their environment and the seasons.

It is the development of our self-awareness and the ability to run our internal dialogue that give us the illusion that we are separate entities. This persistent illusion has led to what we refer to as ego.

It is interesting too that the word ego has gathered a negative connotation around itself. It is not a bad word in itself as it just describes the sense of self. It is when ego is abused in a self-centred manner that it becomes an issue. People would soon stop harming each other if they thought it would be harming themselves.

If you did biology at school, you may have heard about

vestigial organs. These are parts of our anatomy we used in our evolutionary past which have now atrophied to a become remnant. Examples include the skin flap in the lower corner of our eye near our nose. The appendix is another.

You have heard and used phrases like, "It's on the tip of my tongue" or "My heart goes out to you".

We talk about how we 'can feel it in our water' or that our 'gut tells us something'. Our language gives much away about what is really going on in our minds, and our bodies.

There is a conventional view that it is the complexity of the human brain that generates self-awareness.

As we have evolved, the frontal lobes of our brain have taken on the very onerous role of processing not only our thoughts but our feelings.

This is why you may be, "In two minds over something, with your heart telling you one thing and your head the other".

Alternatively, you may find yourself saying, "I think I'll go with my gut on this one."

These utterances are no accident. They are a reflection of what is actually going on in our bodies and minds.

From an evolutionary perspective, our self-awareness was the last feature to develop. It's now become so dominant that we've forgotten about the other mind centers.

Our minds actually inhabit every cell of our body and some think the mind may exist outside our physical form. Our brains act as a sort of central processing unit that generates the illusion of reality based on the input from our primary and sixth senses. Its function is to process and to allow us to think and express ourselves. Such is the dominance of our self-awareness; it's understandable that we've come to believe that our brains and minds are co-sited.

At various points in our body we have conglomerations of aspects of our minds centered on areas like the larynx, the heart and the gut. These are just three of the most well known points in and around our bodies which are also known as chakras. They are like portals to different aspects of the superconsciousness (more on this later) and we have over two hundred of them.

When I was first introduced to the concept of chakras, I thought they were no more than a notion, or at best a metaphor. Imagine my surprise when, with a little training, I found you can 'see' them, sense with them and influence with them.

This next step could be one of the most vital you ever take in tapping into your full creative flow and that's to re-engage with your vestigial mind centers. The good news is that re-connection only takes little time and practice and these mind centers haven't so much atrophied as just been ignored.

It turns out that these centers are much better adapted to processing certain types of thoughts than our brains. When we engage with them, not only do we tap into light bulb moments more easily, but the brain becomes unencumbered and we begin to think much more clearly. Naturally this has benefits in all aspects of life.

This whole subject merits a book in its own right and to keep this simple to understand, at this stage we will concern ourselves with just four of the most useful centers within the body. We will also explore one center which exists just outside the body too.

Starting with a lower point in our body, somewhere just around the navel, is the location of our gut mind. This is the area where we generate our drive and desire to move forward. It is referred to as the solar plexus chakra and is where we generate the fuel for our body. You may often pat it after a good meal. It is also the area best suited to processing thoughts relating to instincts.

Successful business people like Richard Branson and James Caan pride themselves on being in tune with their gut mind, as do inventors like James Dyson and Trevor Baylis.

Next is our heart center, or heart chakra, which unsurprisingly is the location for our feelings and emotions. It provides a rich source of material for any invention and is also a great place to get feedback on the quality of your idea.

You get a warm feeling in your chest when you have your light bulb moment. If you are harboring doubts or fears, your heart centre is eminently more suited to dealing with them than your brain. Quite literally, this is the place to tap into when you really want to love what you are doing.

The next center is located around our larynx and this is the area from which we speak and communicate with the outside world. It is also known as your throat chakra. One useful way of proof reading anything you have written is to read it out loud. If it comes across clearly to your ears, it will read well. If you find you are pausing for breath then you should look at punctuation and sentence structure.

Another key centre within our body is the third eye or pineal gland, which is located pretty much in the center of our brains at the top of the spinal column. This is the place within our bodies where we receive our intuition and inspiration. Learning to listen to it, and to trust it, is essential for anyone engaged in the creative process.

Finally, imagine a point an inch or above your head. This somewhat ethereal point is known as the alpha chakra and it's thought to be the place where your brain-mind connects with the superconsciousness. This is something we will explore more in the next chapter.

I cannot stress enough that it doesn't matter if this is all physically true but, you will make huge leaps forward by merely thinking as if it is. The proof, if needed, is in the pudding of your light bulb moments.

A networking contact of mine called Bill Liao neatly summed this up for me one day when he said, "It only has to be true enough."

A strong connection with your vestigial mind centers is key in assessing and knowing which of the many light bulb moments you have that you should pursue.

So you have within you, and without you, these dormant areas that you can use as an unlimited creative resource.

Your gut can be relied upon to direct you.

Your heart you can tap into for source material and for feedback on how you feel. It will also handle and process your fears.

Your voice allows you to check your words are re-sounding. The use of the hyphen here is intentional.

Your third eye is the communication channel to your conscious mind for the inspiration provided to you by the super-consciousness via your crown chakra to the alpha chakra. In some circumstances, it is also fed ideas directly from the back of the head via the cerebellum.

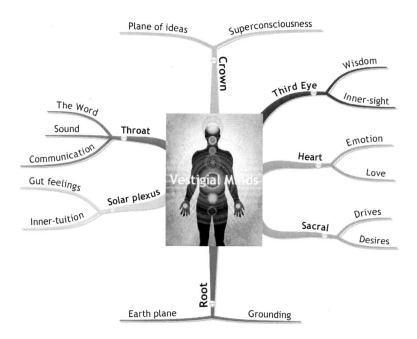

Now this might all sound fantastical or even confusing. How do you go about using these mind centers? How do you know which one is talking to you, and how do you know which one to trust?

The next illumination will help you re-engage with them, but one of the most useful ways is to analyze your own language. By your own language, I refer to your body language, your spoken and written words and your internal dialog. They are your barometers.

Let me give you some examples.

If you ever see me speak, you will often see me grasp the air above my head. I had no idea I did this until it was pointed out to me by a lady who is tuned into auras. She saw me pulling ideas 'out of the ether' into my brain.

Notice where you place your hands when you speak. Sometimes, you pat your chest or hold them over your neck or on your forehead. It is because you are working primarily with that mind center.

Listen to others when they say things like, "Let's sound this out", they are using their larynx centre to test an idea.

So if you do hear someone say, "Off the top of my head ..." it is really worth paying attention to what follows as it is probably the essence of a light bulb moment.

Also, if something is "At the back of your mind", it means something or someone is trying to communicate something to you.

At the end of reading this chapter, which I know might sound a bit out there, you may want to give your left, analytical brain a rest.

Just ask yourself, what does your gut tell you about all this? Is it at least worth investigating and trying out?

## Illumination 5: Re-minding Yourself

What is so wonderful about the plasticity of the brain and the mind is that the patterns we build up that don't serve us can be so easily and quickly replaced by ones that do.

You may have heard it said, "If something doesn't work, then try something else until it does." Marketing is a great example of that.

In a similar vein, Einstein is often quoted as saying, "You cannot use the same thinking that caused the problem to solve it."

By reconnecting with your vestigial minds you achieve three feats at once:

- Your conscious brain frees up for pure ideas and new flavors of thought
- You become more efficient
- Connection to vestigial minds, especially your alpha chakra, gives you access to a rich and unlimited source of ideas.

Connecting to your vestigial minds is much easier to do than you think. This is because the art is only forgotten, not deleted.

It's time to do another Mind Map. You know now that one of the reasons we do this is that it will bypass the conscious critic and allow access to deeper regions of mind.

Start with an image of your idea at the center and draw four branches from it, labeled as overleaf:

- Spin offs
- Likes
- Gut feelings
- Actions

Without thinking, on the Spin Off branch list three or four lateral ideas on sub-branches for how or where else your concept could be applied.

Next, on the Likes branch, add sub-branches as to what you like particularly about them.

Now, add sub branches to Gut Feelings, as to how you feel about the spin off ideas.

Lastly, add sub branches to Actions of what you intend to do about all these ideas, with the specific actions by when and how.

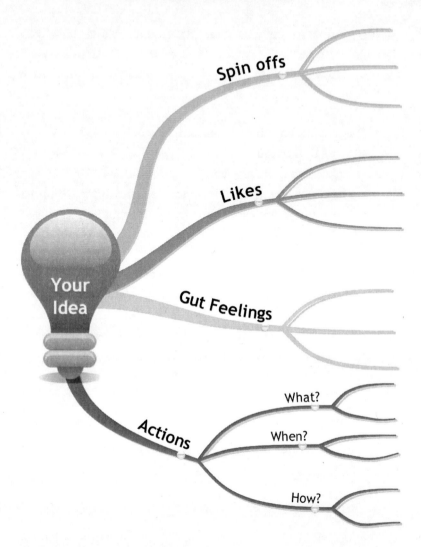

When you have completed the map, look at each branch in turn and reflect on where your consciousness is sited as you read them and when you completed them.

If you want to further strengthen the connection to your vestigial minds, you will find an audio visualization on my web site called Re-minding Yourself.

As you will see in the remaining chapters, by reconnecting to your vestigial minds, you start to become whole and inspired, yet remain immensely grounded.

You enter a state of neo-consciousness, or merged mind, which is something we will explore further towards the end of this book.

## Flashbacks

Our minds are not co-sited with our brains but our main awareness is.

Our vestigial minds operate ahead of our conscious brains and are invariably right.

These minds are merely dormant although somewhat out of touch or atrophied.

It pays huge dividends to get back in touch with them.

6

# Collective Thoughts

*"All the soarings of my mind begin in my blood."*
Rainer Maria Rilke

There have been many times throughout history where two or more people come up with the same bright idea at the same time. Some of these cases will undoubtedly be down to either plagiarism or espionage but some are the result of pure synchronicity of thought and invention.

In this modern day and age, unless you sit in a dark cave, you are bombarded by terabytes of data each day. You could easily scan a newspaper but not consciously read an article about a new invention or idea but then it could appear in your conscious mind sometime later, perhaps as a light bulb moment. You then see the invention mentioned on TV or the Internet sometime later and you might think someone has stolen your idea when it wasn't necessarily yours in the first place.

So it's quite understandable that this sort of thing happens all the time in our so-called connected or wired world. I know of many of the sources of the ideas in this book but I am sure there are others that have percolated their way through my unconscious mind.

This issue is, of course, nothing new. One such case which is as well known for its intense acrimony as much as its significance, is the development of differential calculus, pretty much around the same time, by Isaac Newton and Gottfried Leibniz. Both men were renowned for working in isolation and secrecy and there was no Internet or telecommunications network in those times to leak one scientist's work to the other. Even if there had been espionage, the postal service from Germany to England would take weeks.

Newton went on to use calculus to develop the Theories of Gravitation that we now use to send space probes around the Solar System.

For just one of his next tricks, Leibniz came up with binary notation used by modern day computers. If they had just been friends and collaborators, and didn't waste time arguing about whose idea it was, just imagine what else these two great minds thinking alike might have come up with.

It was another great mind a couple of centuries later, that of Carl Jung's, who popularised a mechanism whereby Newton and Leibniz may have unconsciously communicated. Jung called it the Collective Unconscious. It is also known as the Collective Consciousness. It has many other names too such as the Cosmic Consciousness, the Noosphere, the Morphic Field and Superconsciousness. I prefer the term Superconsciousness as it implies it is a state we can enter as opposed to something which is somehow separate from us.

The concept that there is a collective thought pool is embedded in virtually all religions (although sometimes hidden by nomenclature) and certainly in most mystical traditions.

You will find it called names like Satori, or Brahman, in theological and mystical literature of thousands of years standing, some even refer to it as the 'mind of God'. It has been called the Akashic Records in new age spiritual thought and quantum physics. More recently quantum physicists have dubbed it the Zero Point or Information Field.

Ironically, perhaps, it is our evolution to the state of conscious self-awareness that has disconnected us from our vestigial minds that also separates us from this superconscious source of collective wisdom.

The concept is that all knowledge and wisdom are somehow locked up in a huge memory bank that we can tap into at any time. This includes all past and future thoughts and the 'thoughts' of all living things, not just humankind.

Depending on your belief set, you can also extrapolate this to include all inanimate objects, the Earth, the Moon, planets, stars and perhaps even extraterrestrial life forms.

If you want to read more on the subject, Lynne McTaggart's book The Field is a quite accessible version. Ervin Lazlo's Science and the Akashic Field goes some way to giving it a possible scientific framework.

In summary of the theories around this, it's possible that the collective consciousness is wrapped up in 'higher' dimensions and that our brains are transducers that can not only 'read' from it but 'write' to it. Rather like an ethereal internet.

Purely from the point of view of having light bulb moments on demand, it's a really useful concept to go along with. Especially bearing in mind that we use maps and models to navigate our world and having such an easily understandable model seems to yield practical, real world results.

A good example of how this works across time could be the prescience, or pre-science, exhibited by Leonardo da Vinci that I mentioned earlier. Did he 'invent' the helicopter by seeing someone piloting it in the future? Did he imagine the parachute just in case someone needed to escape from one when it failed?

To get our heads around how to tap into the collective consciousness to access such light bulb moments, we need to replace our left and right hemispheric model of mind with a tiered Three Mind model.

Instead of slicing through the physical brain to look at its function, it's useful to analyze the brain from a mind-full perspective. At the surface layer, we have what we call the conscious mind.

This gives us the illusion of reality, and also seems to have an in-built narrator which sometimes doubles up as an inner critic.

As you are reading these words, try to identify who exactly is reading them and who is making sense of them?

To add a little further mystery, stop reading for a moment and listen to your inner voice. What accent is it speaking to you in?

Apparently it's been measured that the conscious mind can process about seven (plus or minus two) 'things' per second. This is probably why you can remember seven digit phone numbers and, if they are any bigger, you remember the area code as a chunk, like 020 or +00 31.

For much of the time, our conscious mind seems to be either idling or running that internal commentary of what we are thinking. Occasionally we can be replaying a previous encounter or previewing or planning something we are about to say in the future.

So it is your conscious mind which is probably reading these words to you. If so, consider who is reading what and to whom. If you have met me and you know my voice, you may even superimpose it on the words as you read them. You could view the ability to write and read as a form of telepathy.

While all of this is going on, what is also feeding the conscious mind is the unconscious mind which is sometimes referred to as the subconscious mind. It is by definition every-thing we are potentially able to be conscious of but aren't partic-ularly paying attention to at that time.

The unconscious mind primarily takes its input from your five senses of sight, hearing, taste, smell and touch. You will see later that this is not the limit of its inputs.

To show yourself how the unconscious mind works, think about your little finger. This will remind you that you have one. Or, have you ever noticed how you can pick out your name, or that of your favourite football team or rock band, from the background hubbub at a party?

The unconscious mind also regulates conveniently

automated lower level functions such as breathing and your heart beat; you have to work a little to become aware of them and then to control them. Some functions such as blood sugar and hormone levels, for most of us, will always remain out of conscious control.

Your unconscious mind is also the seat of your emotions and the route to accessing all memories. It is said that it processes something like two million bits of information per second. This is a huge number but I suspect it is a gross underestimate. A number closer to infinity is probably a better bet.

Whatever the number though, there is a huge gap between what the conscious and unconscious minds process.

What is clear is that certain types of mental activity block both the conscious and unconscious minds.

Try this. Get a piece of paper and a pen and start thinking of something. Then write it down and notice that at the point you start writing, the thinking seems to stop. When you stop writing, the thinking can start again.

This demonstrates how we flip between thinking and doing. It's as if you can only do one or the other. In fact, when you are writing too, you almost become a reader.

To be creative, your conscious and unconscious minds have to be not only uncluttered but also to be interacting in such a way as to give clear access to your memories and inspirations.

What is actually happening is that our minds are constantly moving from one state of awareness and consciousness to another.

At the cusp between being conscious and unconscious, you are in a mode I call Whole Mind Not-Thinking. To experience light bulb moments on demand, the trick is to get into this not-thinking state where the conscious and unconscious minds are perfectly poised so that creativity can flow.

We need to extend the model a little and introduce the idea that there is a layer of our mind which sits between the unconscious mind and the superconsciousness.

This layer of mind is again one that instinctively we feel we possess. It has many names but we will call it the Higher Self. You could equally call it the Lower Self, the Inner Self or the Outer Self. This is because it sits outside our normal three space dimensions and one time dimension and is the part of our mind that connects us with the superconsciousness ... or more specifically the state of superconsciousness.

The Higher Self can also be thought of as a part of us that acts as our guidance, directing us through our life experiences, both good and bad.

If you accept that the superconsciousness stores all thoughts, this could explain how sometimes you have an idea and don't act on it, only to see someone else come out with your invention a year or so later. How annoying is that! Has someone else tapped into your light bulb moment ... or perhaps you tapped into theirs?

This diagram is a two dimensional representation of how this type of occurrence could come about. You will notice how the conscious mind is surrounded by the unconscious mind, which in turn is enveloped by the Higher Self.

The route to the superconsciousness is via the unconscious mind with the Higher Self being the connector.

At all times, the 'you-in-the-present' is connected to versions of 'you-in-the-past' and 'you-in-the-future'. You are also connected in this way to all other living things.

The Superconsciousness

The Zero Point Field – The Akashic Field
All knowledge, all wisdom, all memories
Outside space, inside time

Someone else or you
*in the past*

You
In the Present

Someone else or you
*in the future*

Note that any negative emotions such as anger, fear and guilt run as gestalts in the unconscious mind and, if present, they will block this communication.

Rupert Sheldrake has almost single handedly promoted and championed the idea of morphic resonance. It explains why starfish can re-grow limbs and how our pet dogs can know when we are coming home. It also goes some way to explain how we can be in tune with our future self as well as our past selves.

We access our past selves through memory. This feels natural as the flow of time in our reality goes in the direction we think of as forward. The way we access 'future memories' is that they appear in our consciousness in the forms of visions, whispers of thoughts and light bulb moments. In essence, we are morphically resonating with ourselves but forwards in the dimension of time.

I cannot stress enough that whether all this exists or not is merely academic, and it is not the aim of this book to begin to prove it or disprove it or explain the science of it. What is remarkable is that just by thinking, or more accurately not-thinking, in this way, produces uncanny results in the inventive process.

Using these concepts, our minds can be tuned into a virtually unlimited source of inspirations. The superconsciousness is the pool from which light bulb moments emanate.

## Illumination 6: Connecting to the Superconsciousness

By far the best way to connect to the superconsciousness is to take up some form of meditative practice.

Now this doesn't mean having to sit cross-legged on the floor in complete silence for an hour each day. Although, if this is for you, there is nothing wrong with that.

I meditate in some form daily but before I started I had no idea how to switch my mind off. There was also no way I could spare even 10 minutes in my busy day. Now I realize, if I don't take the time out to still my mind, I have a worse day and I get less done. You also learn after a while how to 'jump out of time' so you can get four or more hours work done in just an hour.

After a while, you also experience a merging of your Higher Self, unconscious and conscious minds.

There are loads of ways to meditate and this illumination is just to recommend that you take up one or more. I recommend trying a few so you can see what suits you best.

- Sitting upright in a chair for 5 or 10 minutes and focusing on your breath, a candle flame or a spot on the wall - optionally with some light, instrumental background music.
- Walking, ideally in nature, while looking up yet paying attention to the pattern of your foot falls.
- Take up Tai Chi, Chi Gong, Pilates or Yoga.
- Use a meditation CD or meditation machine.

After a while and a little practice what happens is quite amazing. It is not so much that you communicate with the superconsciousness but you become super-conscious by reconnecting with it.

The primary key to unlocking this super-conscious state is via something else we all do fairly naturally and that's breathing.

**Flashbacks**

Assuming that the superconsciousness exists is a great model we can use to postulate the source of light bulb moments.
It is not important whether it exists or not so long as thinking it that might exist generates ideas.
Meditation and quietening the mind is the easiest mechanism to tap into it.

The side benefits of meditation are improved health, well being and also good luck.

It is also completely free and anyone can do it with minimal practice.

# 7

# The In-spirational Breath

*"A mortal lives not through that breath that flows in and that flows out. The source of his life is another and this causes the breath to flow."*
Paracelsus

It might seem incredible but one of the most fundamental things that we all do when we are alive is inextricably wrapped up with our thought processes - and that is to breathe.

Now most people don't realize we speak on the out-breath. Try and speak on an in-breath to see what I mean.

I've mentioned that the phrases like "let me chew that one over" give away what we are thinking and what is actually happening.

In the same way, the derivation of individual words sometimes sheds light on their true meaning and etymology.

Look up the word inspiration in a dictionary and you will see definitions something like this from www.dictionary.com :

- an inspiring or animating action or influence
- something inspired, as an idea
- a result of inspired activity
- a thing or person that inspires
- the act of inspiring
- the quality or state of being inspired
- the drawing of air into the lungs; inhalation

These are all fairly standard and to be expected.

Depending on the dictionary, you may also see definitions such as:

- a divine influence directly and immediately exerted upon the mind or soul
- the divine quality of the writings or words of a person so influenced

These are somewhat unexpected and imply that there is an external influence at work, where perhaps the breath as the agency that carries or modulates it.

The etymology of the word comes from the Latin "in" and "spirare" to breathe. Of course, inspiration is half of the respiration process.

Yet we commonly use the word without connecting it to the breath, as in "she is such an inspiration" or "that view from the top of the hill is so inspiring".

This linguistic disconnection has led to a loss in our understanding.

If we hyphenate the word in-vention, we also see that it is routed in the breath. We are literally 'venting in' ideas – bringing them in with our breathing. In the same way, the word 'prescience' or pre-science also implies that we are experiencing scientific enlightenment before it is known. Our language is littered with such clues.

The role of insight [inner-sight] and intuition [inner-tuition] also plays a starring role in the creative process.

It will come as no surprise then that many meditation techniques are based on the breath. There are literally hundreds of meditative practices and even more people who will tell you that their way is the best. You can even buy iPod-like meditation machines nowadays to induce the meditative state.

No matter what technique you use, and I recommend you try several until you find one that suits you, they fall broadly into two classifications known in the Buddhist tradition as *samatha* and *vipassana*.

In samathic meditation, you can focus on an object like a

candle or a spot on the wall. Alternatively you can repeat out loud or internally a sound known as a mantra, like "OM" or "AUM". More commonly you focus on your own breathing. The different types of meditation combine these three elements into different permutations either in parallel or in sequence.

In vipassanic meditation, you replace the candle, the mantra and the breath with another type of object, namely your own thoughts. This is akin to the process of counting sheep at night to get back to sleep, and the process I referred to as the Quantum Collapse of Thought. Where it differs slightly is that you become an observer of your own thoughts from a different perspective.

It is when you are in the state of vipassana, that light bulb moments occur. If you've experienced a light bulb moment in the past then you did this without perhaps knowing that this state has been known about for thousands of years. Now you know about this, you can learn how to induce this state on demand.

It has been known for many years that our brains emit electro-magnetic energy in the form of brain waves. We are biochemical and electrical beings after all.

In our normal waking state, we are in what is known as beta state with brain waves oscillating between 15 and 30 times a second. There are three other states known as alpha, theta and delta states where the frequency decreases, to just a few times a second, as we withdraw our consciousness from waking reality through meditation and into deep dreamless sleep.

Note the state is only a measurement of what is going on in our brains. It doesn't cause the state of consciousness; it is just an output from it.

You also don't have to be asleep nor have your eyes closed to experience the alpha, theta or even the delta state.

If you have ever driven home without being consciously aware of how you got from A to B, you were in alpha state. Unless, that is, you were on the mobile phone having a conversation, in which case you were probably in beta.

If you are day dreaming almost to the point of nodding off, you are probably in theta state. You can also experience this when out walking especially in nature. If you do drop off, incidentally, you can enter the state known as delta.

In actual fact, we flip between these states continually. If you have ever been in a boring meeting and your mind wanders elsewhere, you are sliding from a waking beta state into an alpha, theta or even delta state. People who are doodling are also inducing this state.

Through samathic meditative practices, you begin to control your entry into the alpha state. Using vipassanic meditation, you can then access theta and even delta states.

When we have a light bulb moment, for a fraction of a second we naturally flip into the vipassanic state.

The key therefore to having light bulb moments on demand is either to enter the vipassanic state via meditation or, even better, while your eyes are open. The easiest way to do this is to enter the state of samatha and then to allow yourself to slide into vipassana.

The ability to enter this state at will sets up the conditions to experience light bulb moments on demand. Like any activity, the more you practice, the better you get at it.

Getting into the habit of meditating each day is the optimum place to start. There are collateral benefits to this too such as health and well being. You also begin to notice and experience synchronous and serendipitous events in your life. What's more, by starting the day with a meditation, you can better enter the vipassanic state for much of the day.

You also start to appreciate that most thoughts aren't necessarily what you think of as your own. As we will see in the next chapter, this can spill over to our sleeping time too.

## Illumination 7: Inhaling Ideas

This illumination is designed so you can do it at any time of the day with your eyes open. You can also use it at the start of the day as part of a meditative practice. It is the breathing equivalent of the cross crawling exercise in Illumination 5. If you feel particularly in-ventive, feel free to combine the two. There is no right or wrong with these techniques, apart from stopping breathing completely or over-exerting yourself.

This whole process can take only five minutes and after a while practicing in private you should be able to do this easily in any situation. For example, it is great preparation before a presentation or for an important meeting.

We primarily breathe in through our nostrils; this is primarily a defence probably against foreign bodies entering our mouths. What we are probably not aware of is that we favour one nostril over another and this changes throughout the course of the day.

There have been some studies that imply that breathing through our left nostril energizes and enriches our right brain and vice versa for the right nostril/left brain. Remember that we are not so concerned about left or right brain function, more that both hemispheres are engaged and the conscious mind is quietened.

Step 1: Breathe 7 times alternately through each nostril. That is 14 times in total starting on the right nostril and switching to the left nostril and so on. If possible, make the out-breath about three to four times as long as the in-breath. Optionally, you can open your mouth on the out-breath. This is priming the ideas pump.

Step 2: Now switch to your normal type of breathing but become aware of your diaphragm. Breathe 7 times taking in at least double the amount of breath in than your norm by really opening your chest and swelling your belly. Again the out-breath should last three to four times the in-breath.

Step 3: Continue this breathing but perhaps a little shallower. Now imagine that on inhalation, the breath starts at the base of your spine and comes right up past your neck, on the outside of the spine right to the top of your head. On the out-breath, it flows back through your neck and down the spine but on inside of your body. Imagine this is circular and rhythmical and the in- and out-breaths should be of roughly equal duration. Do this at least 7 times.

Step 4: While continuing this type of breathing, imagine that on the in-breath, inspirations and ideas are flowing into you. On the out-breath, internally give thanks and appreciation for the insight and intuition they bring. Use the words inner-sight and inner-tuition if you prefer.

Step 5: At the top of the breath, become aware of the still point just before exhalation, imagine the idea drops into your head from the crown chakra. Note that sometimes it comes in when the breath gets to the base of your skull, the cerebellum. This can also be associated with a bit of a jolt; these are true moments of guidance and are worth paying attention to.

At the end of this exercise, note down any inspirations but ideally as central ideas for Mind Maps to allow you to explore them further.

## Flashbacks

The breath is the fuel of inspiration.
Inspiration is one half of the respiration process.
Pay attention to thoughts on the in breath and the still points.
Breathe more deeply than you do normally at least once a day.
The longer you 'deep breathe', the longer you keep breathing.

# 8

# Ordering Your Dreams

*"I encourage you to make friends with your dreams. They want to be heard - all we need to do is listen."*
Davina Mackail from The Dream Whisperer

What better way to be more productive than by using the third of your life when you are sleeping to be creative?

Many artists, scientists and inventors lay claim to their discoveries coming in the form of dreams.

Salvador Dali used to put a spoon under his elbow on the edge of a table around siesta time. As he dozed off, the spoon would clatter to the floor and he would wake up and paint whatever was 'on his mind'.

This time on the cusp of being awake and asleep is known as the hypnagogic point. At that time, the conscious mind is being put to rest and light bulb moments can just pop in unannounced. Dali's method is a little eccentric. Try it by all means for tapping into creativity with an afternoon nap but it's not so recommended for night time sleep because of the disruption it may cause to your natural sleep patterns.

A point which is of much more use, is its opposite, the hypnopompic point which is between sleeping and waking, as you are just waking up. This is because it's the perfect time to remember your dreams prior to their analysis.

When we are asleep, our unconscious mind is in full operation. It is keeping us alive, regulating our body temperature, beating our heart and pumping air into our lungs - sometimes noisily when we snore. I mention snoring as it's something you wouldn't do when you were awake as your conscious mind inhibits behaviour which might embarrass us and annoy others.

Our dreams similarly are full of insight and illuminations that are normally suppressed or inaccessible to our conscious awareness. When we are asleep we are connected to the super-consciousness - and some people think we also are connected to the minds beyond. Accordingly, our dreams are both intangible and etheric by their very nature. If we do remember them, they often leak from our memory during the day and certainly after a few days. That is unless we analyze them and make note - not so much of the detail, but of their significance.

What works really well with respect to tapping into light bulb moments, and the creative process in general, is seeding your dreams to get insight into something you are exploring.

Indeed, I used this technique while writing this very chapter and received an amazing illumination which I will share with you below.

The way to seed your dreams is simply to think of something you would like some insight on as you drop off into hypnagogia. Actually writing a question on a piece of paper and putting it under your pillow works remarkably well.

The trick though is to be able to remember your dreams in the morning. To do this, what you do is spend a little more time in the hypnopompic state. That is to luxuriate a little longer as you wake up, with a view to bringing the essential elements of the dream into your conscious awareness. All in all, it's a great way to start your day anyway.

It then helps to write them down on a notepad by your bed. Once you've captured the dream, next comes the analysis phase. Apart from a bit of fun and research, it's not necessarily helpful to buy a book which contains someone else's interpretations of dreams.

The imagery and metaphors of your dreams are always personal to you as they are seeded by your life experience. If I dream of an alligator it might be because I associate them with handbags not with being bitten by one, for example.

Occasionally the dream may be literal and will not need to be analyzed at all. If this happens to you then great. When writing fiction, I often get the whole of a chapter in detail.

More often, the dream comes in veiled behind this layer of metaphor and allegory. For most of us, dreams come in images, although they can include sounds, colors, language, music and tastes and smells. Numbers can be of special significance too.

The vividness of the dream too is worth making note of. The richer and more intense it is, the more you should pay attention to it. If the dream recurs or the same theme is repeated, then there is undoubtedly a message for you embedded somewhere inside the dream.

The messages in dreams can convey information about our physical or mental health or even warn us about a situation we are in or about to enter that we have unconsciously noticed involves something we are uneasy about.

In the context of inspirations, they can also make us aware of an opportunity and they mirror to some extent what is going on in your waking life.

For example, if you happened to read the chapter in this book about what could block light bulb moments, especially just before you went to sleep, your dreams may reflect that.

So if you want light bulb moments in your sleep, the more you live and breathe inspirationally and surround yourself by inspirational people, the more inventive your dream-time becomes.

As an example of this, I was writing this chapter on my new iPad and asked for a dream that would act as a good case study for the Illumination in this chapter. What I wanted was something I could use to demonstrate how to analyze a dream. Here's pretty much what I got.

## Illumination 8: Interpreting your Dreams

The dream I got was so vivid that I spent about 15 minutes in the hypnopompic state bringing all the elements back into my consciousness as I became fully awake. I then went downstairs and wrote it down on my iPad so I'd be able to recount about it here.

Now there is no way my conscious mind would let me come up with something as weird as this and it's about an invention that I am in no way planning to develop (even if it could be). What's worth noting though that it is just about possible and that I am trained as an electronic engineer so the dream spoke to me in a language I am familiar with.

Here's what came in and note that, as I wrote it down, I can now remember it in detail over 48 hours later without looking at my notes.

> "I found out that there a new [4 bit] microprocessor that could smell. I remembered that I loved propelling pencils but hated the lead always snapping off if you let too much of it out. So I had a light bulb moment to build a propelling pencil that could smell the surface of paper so that when the lead was near it, a motor was driven just to let the perfect amount of lead out so it never snapped off. It also sensed the pressure you were using too so it knew how much lead it could leave exposed."

I think you'll agree, it's maybe a nice to have invention but it's a sledgehammer to crack a nut. I know there are loads of better ways of sensing pressure and proximity like strain gauges and capacitative sensors. There's no need to wait for a microprocessor that can smell. Anyway if one existed, there are loads of much better and relevant applications like checking to see if the contents of your fridge are going off. It continued:

> "So using the same pencil with motor attached, I made an under-water version. Scuba divers could enter a text message and the motor pulsed it out into the water by generating a sonar wave so others

*could pick it up on their pencils. The spin offs for this motorized pencil were amazing. I was going to be able to retire on the proceeds - better wake up and make it happen!!"*

You can see I was being particularly inventive that night - not one but two potential light bulb moments.

In the cold light of day, I do not intend to drop everything and start developing these two inventions - or even a neater way of implementing both ideas. The message had two meanings which can easily be extracted by this simple analysis technique.

On a piece of paper, draw three columns. In the first, list the bullet points of the dream:

- Pencil
- Lead snapping
- Underwater communication

In the second column, list what else they might mean:

- Writing blocked because lead snapping
- Make use of latest technology
- Difficulty in communicating
- Spin offs

Then head up the third column with an opportunity or problem that is current for you - for me it's the iPad and this book. What then comes to mind is:

- The iPad is a brilliant development (like the smelling microprocessor)
- It's the applications though that really makes it tick
- The spin off potential is amazing (underwater SMS)
- Apple developers can benefit so much from their under-lying technology

- I should do an iPad app based on the principles in this book
- This will allow me to communicate the ideas without difficulty to a wider audience
- This in turn will spur on loads of other inventors and generate even more light bulb moments.

Now from the outset, I planned a version of this book that could be read on an iPad (as well as in print) but I hadn't considered modelling the processes in an app quite in this way. But now I am. I may not develop it myself from scratch though, as there are some excellent brainstorming and Mind Mapping apps that I could 'white label' or co-brand. The idea is seeded though.

Apart from any of this, the dream gave me an excellent, real life case study which I could use for this Illumination. To me, that is the tangible benefit of this particular dream.

So your Illumination is to start a dream journal. Optionally seeding your dreams with a note under your pillow. Then wake up slowly letting your dreams come into your conscious world. Finally analyse them using the three column method.

Part 2 of this book is all about making these dreams a reality. Before we get there, there's just a little more thinking about thought to do.

## Flashbacks

Dreams are rich source of light bulb moments.

Most messages come in metaphor and need interpretation.

You can seed your dreams to generate light bulb moments on demand.

# 9

# Flavors of Thought

*"Our thinking should have a vigorous fragrance, like a wheat field on a summer's night."*
Frederick Nietzsche

As I mentioned, when I drew the Mind Map in chapter 3 of the word associations leading from the phrase "light bulb moment", it occurred to me that thoughts came in different flavors ... or even colors.

In the same way as Newton used a prism to separate light into its component colors, we can separate our thoughts into various types. Light also varies in intensity which of course is mirrored and reflected [pun intended] in our language as in phrases like "I've just had this blinding flash of inspiration".

I actually already knew about this but I hadn't considered its application in the context of light bulb moments. Indeed, it made me realize that the light bulb moment itself is a very special flavor, and strength, of thought. The way to taste it is to work through the other flavors as if you are working through a gastronomic meal with the best course being saved for last.

Incidentally, these flavors have a correspondence to the colors of the aura. If you are blessed with the ability to perceive auras, you can tell which mode of thought a person is in by its shape and color. You can also see the thought patterns that emanate from the various vestigial mind centers, as well as seeing external thought patterns entering the auric field.

If you think this sounds weird, so did I before I redeveloped the ability, with just a little training, to be able to do this. In fact, most babies can see auras and you can observe them looking around people rather than at them. It's another example of an ability we lose when we gain self awareness.

Like the colors of the light spectrum, the flavors of thought blend into each other smoothly. They also fall into three main types almost like the primary colors red, green and blue.

Again our language gives us many clues. People 'see red', are 'green with envy' and, hopefully after reading this book, do lots of 'blue sky thinking'.

The classifications our thoughts fit into map into the Three Mind Model as follows:

Conscious mind thoughts:
- Inner dialog and inner critic
- Replay of conversations
- Rehearsing future conversations
- Planning something you are about to do
- e.g. movement in sport, paint, play music

Unconscious mind thoughts:
- Gut feelings
- Fear, guilt, sadness and anger
- Pain, hurt and discomfort
- Memories, especially those that suddenly surface
- Love

Higher Self thoughts:
- Enlightenments
- Knowings
- Intuitions
- Ideas, innovations and inventions
- Dream and day dreams
- Light bulb moments

We spend most of our time flipping between one mode of thought and another. So it is no wonder we are in two or more minds about things when we have to process this lot.

The trick to having light bulb moments on demand is to spend more time having Higher Self types of thoughts. In this state, however, you are in dreamlike kind of world where ideas can have the habit of remaining ethereal and ungrounded. You will see this is where the Science of Light Bulb moments comes in.

Before moving to the next part of the book, it's worth exploring that each flavor of thought has its sub-divisions and its complements. The color red appears in pink, sienna and orange. Blue and green meet in cyan which is the absence of red. The same color mixing parameters used for color of brightness, hue and saturation, apply to thoughts.

You may, for example, have levels of anger ranging from rage through to being just a little peeved. This is akin to the saturation of anger going from vivid red to pale orange. Your anger might really be annoyance or a feeling of being let down, which is like the hue ranging from reddish-blue (ie. purple) to reddish-green (ie. yellow).

Light bulb moments come in different intensities or saturations. They range from the intense which is almost like a spiritual awakening experience. You may feel compelled to drop everything and pursue it with every resource at your disposal. This level of light bulb moment can affect you physically too.

It may alternatively just be a whisper. You know you're on to something but you are not sure what it is yet. It's on the tip of your tongue or at the back of your mind.

They also come in different hues or types. You have probably heard or met people who are clairvoyant or psychic. To me this isn't a special gift; it's something we all possess to one degree or another.

Receiving a light bulb moment is akin to seeing the future. You could envisage it as being a message from your future-self.

Different people receive these messages in different ways.

They are sometimes referred to as the "clairs". I ascribe no paranormal significance to them as I regard them as a state of mind which is completely normal but perhaps not explored or contextualized correctly. Often this is called sixth sense and it appears we all have six of them. Just try saying "six sixth senses" though.

The six sixth senses are:

- Clairvoyance - seeing
- Clairsentience - feeling
- Clairaudience - hearing
- Clairolfactory - smelling
- Clairgustatory - tasting
- Claircogniscence - knowing

Each of them can be developed together or separately by various exercises, primarily though via meditation.

The sense which is most relevant to experiencing light bulb moments is claircogniscence. This is where you not only get access to information you weren't previously aware of, but you also know it is the right course of action for you.

That said, if you are a musician or an actor, you may favor clairaudience. A painter will have stronger clairvoyance. A parfumier will be able to invent smells in their mind through a strong clairolfactory sense. A chef, or gourmand, is able to imagine tastes using their clairgustatory organs of perception.

You have probably experienced a time when you are in the flow. Perhaps you have a run of luck with gambling, or clients, referrals and opportunities just appear from nowhere. This is when your claircogniscence is at work.

The converse is when things just don't go your way. Nothing works, nothings sticks, problems are insurmountable. Your flavors of thought turn to reflectivity, inner criticism, frustration and even anger.

Now, is the cart before the horse or the tail wagging the dog? As Iain McGilchrist puts in his book, who exactly is in charge, The Master or his Emissary?

Quite simply, to change your world, you just have to change your way of thinking and the flavor of your thoughts. By doing this, you can be in the mode that light bulb moments are the norm and not random.

Looking back at the previous chapters now, you will see how the first part of this book guides you towards this point.

First we looked at what a light bulb moment is and what stops them.

Next we looked at the function of our left and right brains and how to get into the Whole Brain Thinking state.

We were then re-minded that brain doesn't equal mind and mind is not the brain. There may be states of mind and consciousness that exist outside our physical bodies and indeed our physical world ...

... noting that these are just models to help us tap into light bulb moments.

Then we explored the importance of breath in the process of in-spiration and as a tool to quieten the conscious mind.

Then we looked at the importance of the waking dream-like state and the ability to program and analyse dreams in the context of creativity.

Finally, that our thoughts come in flavors and we can choose which ones we want to experience.

You now have a whole armory of tools at your disposal to generate unlimited light bulb moments.

The real skill is being able to manifest them into our physical reality so you capitalize on them.

Before moving to Part 2 of the book, The Science, this last illumination takes you on a simple mind journey around the flavors.

## Illumination 9: Shifting Thoughts

Observing eye patterns is not only useful in determining the flavor of thought that someone's experiencing. By moving your eyes in one direction or another, you actually enter that way of thinking.

You can experience this in two ways; with eyes closed or with eyes open.

First I'll take you through the eyes closed method. Obviously you'll have to read this and remember it before you do it.

Think of an opportunity you would like to explore - say a light bulb moment that's not fully formed yet.

Then close your eyes and for 30 to 60 seconds, reflect on it but with your eyes pointing in these directions and thinking in these flavors.

Flavor 1: With your eyes directed towards bottom right reflect on how you feel about the opportunity. You can even ask your gut and heart minds for their input and notice what comes back in response.

Flavor 2: Now move your eyes to the bottom left and listen to your inner voice, almost asking yourself what it thinks about the opportunity. You may get an answer in an image, as an actual voice or a knowing. Some people even experience tastes or smells.

Flavor 3: Move your eyes now top left and think back to times when you have developed a similar opportunity. What experiences did you have than that might be applicable in this case so either you don't repeat similar errors or you execute this one even better?

Flavor 4: Lastly move your eyes top right and imagine all the possibilities and spin offs for this opportunity.

Now take these imaginings and turn them up a few notches. Make them brighter and more colorful. Make them fizz and bristle with possibilities. Imagine the sounds associated with them are louder and more harmonious.

When you open your eyes, you may like to write these down. If so, use the Mind Map template below.

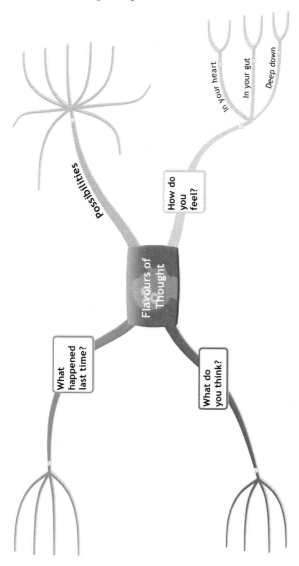

Note that if you want to do this exercise in a business context where getting everyone in the room to close their eyes might be embarrassing, this is a great business tool for idea storming. The equivalent eyes open method is simply doing the Mind Map. If you make sure that the branches follow this pattern, then if you project it on a big screen, it will induce a similar effect.

You can use this eyes open method privately too. Feel free to combine this illumination with others in this section, especially the cross crawling and breathing techniques, for even better results.

I look forward to the day where all business meetings use these techniques as a warm up exercise. Apart from all the inspirational benefits, it's a great ice-breaker and a fabulous ego suppressor. You will see in Part 2 that suppression of ego is not so much about managing personalities but directing thought so it can be put to better use.

## Flashbacks

Not all thoughts are the same in type or quality.
Not all thoughts are necessarily our own.
You can tune into different flavors of thought.
With a little practice, you will be able to easily pick out the light bulb moments from the general noise floor.

# Part 2

# The Science

*"Although this may seem a paradox, all exact science is dominated by the idea of approximation."*
Bertrand Russell

If you've been taking the Illuminations in Part 1, you may have experienced one or more Aha-moments already. It's equally possible that you've had a light bulb moment at random, as you've been going about your daily life. Such is the nature of these gifts of inspiration. Just by being alive, on each breath, you have been stirring up and interacting with the collective mind.

So this section is designed to help you take these ideas to the next stage. The 'Science' here does not relate to our neurology or to an explanation of consciousness or ideas. Rather, it describes a methodology which is easy to follow that will help you bring your ideas into physical reality.

Perhaps you had a brainwave but you didn't follow it up, only to see someone else bringing it out a year or two later. Well, this section will guide you through an easy to follow process to prevent this eventuality from happening again.

Incidentally, the exercises in this section are dubbed Crystallizations as they bring Illuminations into physical reality.

You can think of the superconsciousness as a super-saturated solution of thoughts. Our brains are the transducer that taps into them. Our minds and bodies are the vehicle by which we manifest them into our world.

To make this manifestation happen, we will use a process akin to the Scientific Method and indeed show how you can define your own method.

Now we can be forgiven for thinking that the scientific method is something that was developed relatively recently - say since the Industrial Revolution.

In fact, it has been in common use for thousands of years. It's often said that Aristotle was its progenitor but who actually introduced it has been lost in antiquity. It's more likely that it fell into common usage because any other methods led to less successful results.

It is essentially common sense. If you think about it, it's how we are programed to learn from the moment we leave the womb.

Here's how it works in essence:

Step 1: You observe or notice a new phenomenon, or a pattern, and you try and make sense of it.

Step 2: You form an explanation, theory or hypothesis. This can take the form of an analogy like "riding a beam of light" or a mathematical equation like $E=mc^2$.

Step 3: You make a prediction based on your theory.

Step 4: You measure and test against your prediction.

Step 5: If it's successful, you shout "Eureka" and if not you go back to Step 1 or 2.

Using this technique is how a baby learns that making certain sounds attracts attention to get fed or a change of nappy.

For scientists, what then happens after Step 5 is that your discovery then becomes a "Law" that is until someone else (or you) finds something that doesn't fit the model. The whole sequence is then repeated again and again.

By using these techniques, we have developed a remarkable understanding and mastery of our physical world. By probing the very small and the very large, we understand how matter and energy behave and interact. Devices we use daily in the modern world would look like magic to anyone journeying to our time from even 50 or 100 years ago.

We can tap into a huge library of much of human knowledge within seconds. We have devices that can see inside our bodies and some say our minds. We can zap cancerous cells without making an incision.

Using Laws derived by Newton using the scientific method 400 years or so ago, we are able to send images back from space probes orbiting other worlds millions of miles away from the Earth. Even without using later modifications like Einstein's Theory of Relativity, Newton's Laws of Motion are accurate enough to ensure a probe arrives to within a few tens of metres of its target and within seconds of its planned arrival time. The lack of resistance in the vacuum of space helps here.

Of course light bulb moments occur at all stages of the scientific method - they don't just have to kick the process off.

In step 1, the new noticing of the new phenomenon might be a light bulb moment in itself. For example, noticing an anomaly in some data or seeing the world upside down.

In step 2, as did Newton, Kekulé and Einstein, you conceive of a new way of describing or understanding the world. This could come in a dream or a reverie under an apple tree.

In step 3, your prediction can come in the form of a light bulb moment. For example, if it is true that gravity can bend light, then if there is a solar eclipse, we should be able to see stars that should be behind the Sun during an eclipse. Note that this was predicted by Henry Cavendish as far back as 1784 and proved by Sir Arthur Eddington on the West Coast of Africa in 1919.

In step 4, when your prediction is proven true, the ramifications hit you and the spin off implications are immense. When Watson and Crick determined the structure of DNA, they might not have realized it could be used for forensic uses in catching criminals years later.

If you have a light bulb moment of the form of Step 2 or 3 at any time, you would then jump back to Step 1 to check it and move directly to Step 4 to predict where this might lead.

The people who capitalize benefit from the scientific method fall into three broad camps.

Firstly, the theoreticians who love the pursuit of academic enquiry. For them, being the first to come up with the theory is reward enough.

Secondly, the developers who take the theory and make use of it. Edison was a prime example. Edison was a master at using the scientific method, sometimes in a spectacular showman-like manner. For example, he was a great proponent of Direct Current (DC) over Alternating Current (AC). To show how dangerous AC would be in the home, he electrocuted a circus elephant called Topsy (who had gone mad and killed several of its keepers). Quite an extreme way of testing a hypothesis, I think you'll agree.

Thirdly, people who experience the initial idea in action can have light bulb moments of their own. Customers, observers, competitors and plagiarists can make use of the development in a way the inventor did not foresee. By the way, not all such extensions of the original discoveries are beneficial to absolutely everyone. The electrocution of Topsy led to the development of the electric chair which is still in use today for execution.

In the commercial world, the smart move is to communicate across all three of these types of user. By canvassing users, you can get ideas for the next phase of research and development.

Technology companies like Apple and Facebook even get their users working on new developments on their behalf. The most successful applications for the Apple iPhone and the Facebook social community have every chance of being embedded into future versions. This eventuality can be a source of annoyance or pleasure for any developer. They could either think that their idea has been copied or be proud that their ingenuity was worthy of such an accolade. The smart ones of course either get rewarded financially in some way, perhaps with an offer of employment.

I mention this as the creative path is not necessarily one that is smooth. There have been many cases of copyright theft and commercially naive inventors who see someone else capitalizing on their ideas.

This section contains some light bulb moments and hypotheses of my own to help you benefit from your own genius.

The proof is in the puddings of your in-ventions.

## *10*

# The Cascade of Creativity

*"Creativity is the defeat of habit by originality."*
Arthur Koestler

If you were introduced to the idea of the atom at school, in all probability, you would have been told the atom had a nucleus with electrons revolving around it - much like our Sun and its orbiting planets.

If you continued further study, as I was fortunate enough to do, this would have been replaced as a model by one where the nucleus and its components and the orbiting electrons were really waves of potential and probability - not particles at all.

The particle model emerged in the 19th century only to be replaced by the wave model in the 20th century. In the 21$^{st}$ century, the main advancement will be the integration of consciousness into both models.

Modern day students can of course be introduced to all models and see them in context in just a few short years. This then allows the next wave of understanding to be introduced by a new generation with new perspectives and new light bulb moments.

Even with an understanding of the quantum world, I still prefer to envisage the atomic model as a world of particles - as I am sure perhaps secretly so do many physicists. Indeed many advances in modern day chemistry were achieved using this mode. It still has many uses.

Similarly, well before the periodic table of the elements was discovered, the world was thought to consist of four (or five) elements - namely Ether, Fire, Air, Water and Earth. Traditional Chinese medicine, and other forms of complementary therapies, still use it as one of their fundamental bases.

As a young scientist, inducted to the atomic model, like many I treated the notion there might only be Four Elements with some derision. Latterly however, I've found it has a real practical use - certainly in the context of light bulb moments.

Integrating it into modern day physics may even uncover where all that missing Dark Matter and Dark Energy is hanging out - but that's yet another book entirely.

From the perspective of grounding light bulb moments, using the Four Element model works really well and allows a variant of the scientific method to be applied to them. Actually one of the greatest benefits of the scientific method is its application to so many non-scientific situations. Such malleability is a testament to how much it is based on common sense and, in essence, the fabric of the Universe.

The Four Element model, as is the particle and wave atomic model, is a wonderful metaphor to allow us to better understand our Universe.

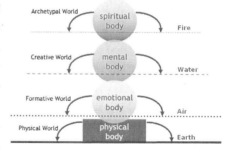

As you can see, the Four Elements map into four worlds. Namely the Archetypal World, the Creative World, the Formative World and the Physical World.

The Archetypal World is the plane of ideas and the source of light bulb moments. It maps neatly into step 1 of the scientific method where something grabs your attention. The element of Fire relates to the raw energy trapped within the universal mind-stuff that we tap into and unleash.

The Creative World is the plane of patterns where thoughts crystallize. Step 2 in the scientific method is where new hypotheses arise. It's associated with the element of Water as this represents the fluidity of thought. It's just an idea we haven't yet formulated but we are working on.

The Formative World is the plane of processes. This is Step 3 of the scientific method where we test the theory and work out what it relates to. The element Air here denotes that the breath is what drives our thinking processes. Without it there is no inter-action.

Lastly the Physical World is represented obviously by the element of the Earth which in turn means physical matter. In step 4 of the scientific method, our theories become real and grounded.

Again, I emphasize this model is just a metaphor but what it points towards is a process whereby our light bulb moments can be grounded into reality.

During the 20th century, several luminaries came up with other similar processing systems. By looking at them briefly, we can see that this type of process can be applied in many situations.

Walt Disney used the concept of Three Rooms in his film production.

In room 1, everyone could come up with the most amazing dreams for the production. No criticism was allowed to sneak in.

In room 2, the dreams were assembled into a storyboard - now used ubiquitously in film production.

In room 3, the inner critics were allowed to have full reign and be externalized. It was just the overall project and no individual that was the subject of the scrutiny.

Later that same century, Edward de Bono, a proponent of lateral thinking, came up with a system of parallel thinking known as Six Thinking Hats.

This has been rolled out in many organizations around the world, both large and small. Not only does it produce amazing results but it reduces meeting times significantly. The main reason for this is that it gives focus and removes egotistical posturing from proceedings.

The group works on an issue with a different colored hat on in turn - which can be a physical hat or an imaginary hat.

The Blue Hat is concerned with control and is initially used to define the topic to be dealt with.

The White Hat is next and deals with what is known already - just the facts, no conjecture. If you don't know something then you note down that is it a fact that you don't know it as opposed to making a guess. This way it gets picked up as an action by the facilitator later.

The Red Hat allows the air to be cleared and everyone's emotions and feelings to be tabled. This is a brilliant hat to don as it allows everyone to vent their anger, fears and frustrations.

Next comes the Black Hat which allows critical judgment to be applied. Most often the negatives of the situation get aired here.

Once these three hats have been used, there is no space for negativity or fear. The space is cleared for creativity to be unleashed, much as we did in the second Illumination.

The Yellow Hat is next and the positives of the venture are brought to the fore.

The next hat is my personal favourite which I wear most of the time as a matter of course. The Green Hat allows 'blue sky' thinking to be unleashed. This is the brainstorming hat.

Incidentally I would have renamed some of them but I'm not Edward de Bono and I am sure he had his reasons.

With the Green Hat on, no idea is deemed unworthy and no other type of thinking - either negative, fearful or critical - is allowed to surface. Egos are nicely suppressed.

Finally, the Blue Hat is worn again to bring the meeting to a close and to summarize actions, roles and responsibilities going forward.

Both Walt Disney's and de Bono's systems generate real world tangible outputs - even more so when combined with the techniques in the first half of this book.

What's clear is that by breaking a task down into component

parts, it becomes manageable and encourages new thinking.

What happens if you skip a step is that nothing gets done and you are just swamped with ideas that never see the real world. In the Four Element model, what happens is that they get as far as the Creative World but then leak back to the superconsciousness.

What you have done is to stir the collective mind up and someone else can now download what was your idea (or so you thought) and annoyingly bring it to market while you are busy on the 'next best thing'.

As a final example in this chapter, I'd like to show you how you can use these models to create and tailor a new model for your own uses and perhaps to map neatly on to an existing process in your organization.

**Crystallization 10: Making your own method**
So while planning this book, I had the light bulb moment that there must be a correlation between the Four Elements, our vestigial minds and the scientific method. And wouldn't it be a neat idea if I brought them together, by way of explanation, by creating a 'new' system of parallel thinking ideal for grounding light bulb moments.

In addition, if it was really simple and memorable, it would have more chance of being adopted and executed.

The IDEA method came to my mind in a flash where:

- I stands for Inspiration
- D for Dream
- E for Evaluate
- A for Actualize

Of course this is simply a variant of Walt Disney's Three Rooms and de Bono's Thinking Hats.

As well as a neat acronym, IDEA can be expressed in a diagram which shows how inspirations cascade down into the physical plane.

They say of course that a picture tells a thousand words and this one sums up this chapter of around 1300 words neatly. In addition, you can see how the Three Mind Model also fits into

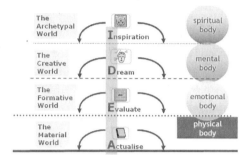

it with the supercon-sciousness as the upper overarching layer.

So your crystal-lization now is to take one of your **Inspir-ations** and apply this model to it as follows:

**Dream** of all the ways you can exploit your idea
**Evaluate** the upside (and downside) of implementation
**Actualise** it of them by assigning timescales and resources to making it a reality.

Then to compound the learning, either apply the IDEA model to another area of your life or come up with your own common yet meaningful word for a process you would like to streamline and make it into an acronym where each letter augments the root meaning.

**Flashbacks**

For light bulb moments to crystallize, a logical and repeatable process must be applied to them.
Parallel thinking neutralizes ego.
By taking time out to do some due diligence, you save much heartache later on.

## 11

# Getting in Sync

*"Anyone can be a millionaire, but to become a billionaire you need an astrologer." –*
John Pierpont Morgan

I mentioned before that the best light bulb moments are not just cracking ideas but they seem to come along at just the perfect moment in time.

The converse situation, as happens perhaps for the majority of people, is that the timing never seems to be just right. Perhaps you are too busy to do anything about your invention or you just don't have the financial resources or haven't met the right backer or partner. Worse still, you might go from day to day with a paucity of ideas.

This can make it even more gruelling when you see someone else seemingly float through life and bring your invention into the world before you've taken a breath.

Now our modern day calendar has much to answer for in the way it has helped us get out of natural time. In the Western world, we have months of unequal length. The seventh, eight, ninth and tenth months of September, October, November and December were usurped by the interlopers of July and August. We have the two Caesars to thank for that as they threw the later months out in favour of their own. Augustus Caesar's month of August at first only had 30 days compared to Julius's 31 day month of July. So that people wouldn't think of him as a lesser emperor, he borrowed a day from the month of February which to this day remains the shortest month of the year.

The other facet of our lives that helps us get 'out of time' is electric light. If you visit any casino in Las Vegas, you won't see a clock anywhere. The lack of natural light means you don't know what time of day it is and how long you have been gambling. You get a similar shock if you go to a cinema in the day time. The film may transport you through different times of the day and indeed different time zones or even different worlds. When you emerge somewhat entranced into sunlight, you can be a little disorientated.

The conspiracy theorists might be tempted to say that the modern day calendar was brought about for the purposes of control. To me, it's more like a big game of Chinese Whispers with dates. Down the ages, it's been tinkered with and adjustments added, like the odd leap second now we have atomic clocks.

Now there's probably nothing we can do as individuals to change any of this. We can however easily run our own personal calendar system which is geared towards grounding light bulb moments.

The first time period to embrace is that of the year with its seasons. Looking back over the last few years, I've noticed I've written and published a new book each year. Now I didn't plan this, and I have only just realized it, but they've all been started in late April and the first draft finished in June. I had been thinking about each book for a while though, and testing out the concepts.

What's even stranger is that the publishing routes all kind of appeared without a huge effort on my part. The publisher of this book, for example, came up in conversation with three different people in the same week who didn't know I was writing a book. Within a couple of weeks of my submission, I was given the green light with the ignominy of rejection letters nowhere in sight.

So if we were to superimpose the IDEA acronym on the seasons, it might look like this (for me at least):

- Inspiration - Summer
- Dream - Autumn
- Evaluate - Winter
- Actualize - Spring

It's worth noting the mnemonic we use for changing the clocks is "Spring forward and Fall back". Incidentally the novelist Kurt Vonnegut proposed that there should be two additional seasons. A two week period between Autumn and Winter called the Locking; and a two week period between Winter and Spring called the Unlocking.

We should also remember that the seasons change with our location on the planet. For those in the Arctic or Antarctic Circles, the absence and presence of light for so many months of the year, I am sure will have a bearing on creativity.

Some individuals are afflicted by Seasonal Affective Disorder - aptly abbreviated to SAD. For them, the seasons and lack of light affect more than just creativity, namely their ability to function.

Likewise, the heat in the Tropics might make it too physically uncomfortable to work. This could well be why, before the age of air conditioning, advances in culture, industry and technology primarily came from the temperate zones.

So it feels natural that Spring is a great season to be starting or crystallizing a project. This is not much use though if you want to do more than one project a year. I suppose if I wanted to write more than one book a year, I could move to the Southern Hemisphere for six months of the year.

Most professional project managers will be aware of the week number that we are in. Personally I wouldn't have a clue. They would also know intimately how many 'man-days' were used, and how many are left, in a project. For them, time would be linear with no rhythm, broken only by weekends and Bank Holidays but largely mapped out across months in the calendar -

or a Gantt chart, after Henry Gantt.

As mentioned, the months we work to are not real. If you were to look at the Earth from Mars, nothing is detectable that denotes months even exist.

There is one big thing, however, that does beat consistent time that a Martian could see and that's the Moon.

It's the closest astronomical object to us yet, if you asked most people, they couldn't tell you the current Moon phase - not least its distance from the Earth and in which direction it was moving relative to them. It's almost too much in our faces.

From Mars however, with a modestly sized telescope and several million miles of objectivity, Moon Time would be obvious.

Any Martian would be able to tell you that the Earth has 13 lunar months a year and they are all about 28 Earth rotations long (that's a day to you and me) - give or take one or two.

Now many vintners and farmers have twigged that the Moon has a significant effect on their crops. Sailors are very respectful of the Moon phase as their lives might depend on the height and power of the tide.

Astrologers are somewhat derided by their observance of the Moon phase. One day astrologers and astronomers will compare notes and find there is more common ground than they thought - and several light bulb moments to emerge from knowledge sharing that would follow.

This is not news but it was known in ancient times that the Four Elements map into the Moon Phase. This means, if we map the Cascade of Creativity to the Moon, our light bulb moments can be developed to a natural time.

Now there are two reasons why this works. Either the Moon is having an affect on our consciousness or it's acting as a big reminder in the sky that we should work through our concepts in a logical manner. If it works, it's academic if either or both of these is in operation. If you are interested in investigating the

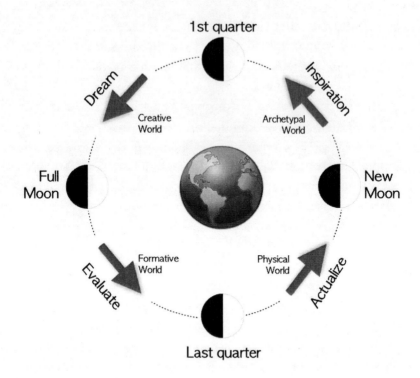

esoteric explanation, then what may be happening is that the Moon is interacting in some way with the Akashic Field around the planet. A more physical explanation perhaps is some kind of tidal pull on the water in our cells.

Now this doesn't mean you can only have a light bulb moment at a certain time but, if you phase your creative projects to the Moon, they will potentially flow much easier.

So this now means you can complete 13 projects a year, not just one or two. If it's a big project, by syncing its creative aspects to natural Moon time, you will get more done and you will get it done more easily.

The same applies to marketing initiatives too. Give it a go as there is no harm in trying. Since I started using the Moon phase to time my workshops, they seem to fill much more easily and generate more creative output for the attendees.

Now this is all well and good but what happens if you have a deadline to adhere to today or this week. You look at your Moon chart and find it's in the wrong phase. Does this mean that all creativity is put on hold?

The point of syncing to natural time is not that becomes a cross to bear but that it's helpful. It is unhealthy for any system or dogma to superimpose itself such that it impedes rather than assists. This would only have the effect of light bulb moment suppression in any case.

Moon phase is just a guide for projects that work to a monthly cycle much as the seasons modulate projects that span over a year or so.

From a day to day perspective, we resort to a diurnal clock. Without thinking about it, we all know when we are most productive. For some, it's that magical time in the morning before the work day kicks in. For others, it's that golden hour when the kids finally go to sleep and quiet descends on the household.

Likewise, there are times when creativity just won't flow. Just after a hearty lunch you can be in the most engaging of presentations or meetings, yet be struggling to keep your eyes open.

The working day is another example of a 'man-made' clock to which we find ourselves adhering in the so-called 'modern world'. Ask any sailor and they will tell you that our natural rhythm is about four hours awake interspersed with a snooze.

From the perspective of generating light bulb moments, these can happen at any time. Indeed, they are just as likely to occur while you are daydreaming or sleeping as when you are awake - certainly in the hypnagogic and hypnopompic times between.

From the purpose of capitalizing and working on the light bulb moment, there is no point pushing water uphill. We should discover our optimum time for being creative and map it out in our diaries.

Having said all of this, there is nothing wrong with working when the Muse takes you. If you do this though, it may be worth noting when these times occur as you may find a rhythm all of your own.

**Crystallization 11: Creativity Journal**

To work out when you are most productive and to better plan your time going forward, there is nothing better than keeping a journal.

You can do this in a simple notebook or using an online diary. Some paper diaries even have the Moon phase in them. If you are a bit of a techie geek like me, you can even find an iPhone app with phases of the Moon and the ability to make notes against them.

In this crystallization, first go back in time and as accurately as you can make notes of when you started and completed projects with an element of creativity over the last year or two. Try and spot patterns in the timings.

Then going forward in your journal, make a note of the following:

- Times and dates when you were creative
- Times and dates when nothing seemed to happen
- Any times when you had a light bulb moment
- Times when unexpected good luck came your way

If you can keep this up for about three months, that should be enough time to see the patterns emerging.

What also happens is that by making notes in this manner, you start to have more light bulb moments and more good luck seems to come your way.

You can keep the journal going indefinitely or, in time, you can also work intuitively, as I do, and just go with the flow.

If I ever find words or ideas aren't coming naturally, I don't fight it. I am fortunate enough to live in the countryside and have two very willing dogs that will oblige with a walk at the drop of a hat.

If you are stuck in an office environment and need a quick burst of inspiration, make a reason to get up and stretch your legs, or you can also do the breathing exercise through alternate nostrils.

## Flashbacks

There is a natural flow to creativity.
There is nothing wrong with not being creative all the time.
It is different for all of us and for different types of project.
When you discover yours, your life will become much easier.
Don't push water uphill.

## 12

# The Importance of Grounding

*"The first 90% of the code accounts for the first 10% of the development time. The remaining 10% of the code accounts for the other 90% of the development time."*
The 90:90 Rule from Tom Cargill

Software development projects are notorious for going over budget and being late. Some also fail to even deliver against user expectation. There are, of course, also reports of massive overspends in other projects in construction and defence.

Oddly enough some projects like major road works and World Cup or Olympic Game stadiums seem to happen on time. One of the reasons for the former is that there are financial incentives for finishing early. For the latter, there is a cut off date which isn't going to move.

Having this same sense of urgency, or a deadline, is great but in the field of light bulb moments, such external pressures tend to dampen creativity.

Fortunately there's a better way. If you look at projects that go awry, there are several repeating factors:

1. The specification changed mid-project - this is known as feature-creep and can come from the inventor, the project team or from clients.
2. External conditions changed - e.g. a change in exchange rate making the product too expensive to produce.
3. Something unforeseen occurred - e.g. a key person left the project.

4. The concept was flawed, it didn't work or the market hadn't been tested and people didn't like it.

5. Someone beat you to it, a competitor came out with a similar (but better) product.

Now when Apple first introduced the Apple Macintosh in the 1980s - swiftly emulated by Microsoft with Windows - they introduced the term WYSIWYG – pronounced "whizzy wig".

It stands for What You See Is What You Get. It refers to the image on screen matching the printed output. As a result, desktop publishing arrived - on our desktops.

When I first got involved heavily with software development, I learned the hard way that projects can get out of control so I looked around for a solution. I came across a system called the Unified Modelling Language [UML] which allowed you to specify a project such that a techie developer could know exactly what to build - and quote for. The outputs from adopting a UML methodology were diagrams that the client could easily understand and sign off.

This was brilliant but not half as good as another acronym that I picked up on my UML training course - and that was IKIWISI - pronounced "Icky Whizzy".

It stands for 'I Know It When I See It' and it's a wonderful mnemonic to bear in mind when you are crystallizing your light bulb moments.

One of the issues that occur with light bulb moments is that, when you experience one, it changes your body chemistry. You get excited and want to drop what you were working on in its favor. At that time, common sense can fly out of the window too - and that's where an IKIWISI approach most comes in handy.

It's irrelevant if your idea is for a software product or a mechanical device, a board game or a new service from your company. The methodology used in software development applies.

As well as our cognizance, we are equipped with visual, auditory and tactile senses. While we can interpret and comprehend a paper-based specification, there is no substitute for being able to see and experience an actual product or service. If it's a new recipe or perfume, we'll use our taste and smell, of course.

## Market Research

The first task in grounding your light bulb moment is to do some market research. Although certain aspects of your in-vention may be entirely new, almost certainly some one has done something similar before. With the Internet, you can search on similar concepts and prior art in seconds and even access patent files online.

You might want to buy products that might compete or to experience similar services to see what's good about them and how your idea might be even better.

You also might want to talk to potential customers and users, perhaps using an NDA [non-disclosure agreement] to protect your idea.

Through this due diligence, you may find someone has just beaten you to it but you get a spin off idea that's even better - sometimes from a potential user.

For example, I nearly wrote a book that would have been a virtual copy of a book that already existed. I wasn't aware of it and it even had the same title that I was planning.

A simple search on Google or Amazon was all that I needed to do. What actually happened was that I met the author and she gave me a copy of her book, not even knowing what I had been planning.

As a result, I didn't overlap her book, I wrote a book that had a completely different approach, and was individual in content and style.

**Proof of Concept**

The second task in grounding your light bulb moment is to create a proof of concept or prototype. This might be a taster session for a service, a space model of a physical product or a software wire frame.

Below is an example of a 'fictitious' screenshot for an iPad application which took minutes to do. A whole application such as this can be scoped in a day or two.

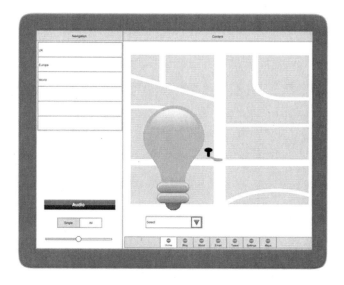

You can then show your model to the people you want to build it and the people you want to promote it, sell it and buy it.

They can give their input early on into the project's inception, which can avoid much wasted time later on. They will 'Know It' and 'See It' for the truly amazing innovation that your light bulb moment has become.

If they don't get it, then you will learn something in an inexpensive and much less painful manner than having taken it to full production.

Now I know this is all common sense but I am amazed at the number of entrepreneurs who get carried away and spend loads of money on marketing ahead of finding out for sure if the market exists for their 'brilliant' product.

## Alpha Testing

The next step is to build another version of the product with some of the functionality of the final product. This can even be tested by team members or clients in confidence. In software industry, this is known as alpha testing.

Here you may even have known bugs or be seeking input on whether the buttons should be gold or pink. You almost want to encourage the tester to break it so you can uncover any flaws in design at an early stage.

You can also test the market for price sensitivity too.

## Beta Testing

From the alpha testing, you incorporate feedback and then come up with a pre-production version of the product or service. You then beta test it to iron out any wrinkles before it goes into production and delivery.

In the beta testing phase, you can use real customers and also solicit some testimonials and reviews that you can use in marketing. You might even make some sales at early adopter prices to help with cash flow.

If you haven't done so already, this is the point where you create all the documentation like the user manual and the sales page on the web. Issues like copyright, patents and other intellectual property are easier to establish once you have this first mover advantage.

Something slightly more esoteric happens as the idea moves out of the archetypal plane of ideas into the material world. It has the tendency to prevent the idea occurring to someone else, in a light bulb moment manner at least. Note, if it's a very good idea, there are no guarantees that someone somewhere won't start emulating your concept.

Note though, that to avoid such copy cat tendencies you also have to be sure not to be fearful of this eventuality occurring. If your idea does get copied then, it's because another mechanism is in operation.

Once you move into production, the idea becomes real. The inventor can then either focus on something new or on improving and capitalizing on spin off ideas based on the original invention.

**Crystallization 12: The last 10%**

There are many reasons why the last 10% of the project seems to take 90% of the time and resources.

The first is completely psychological. When you are 'in the zone' flushed with that cocktail of exciting biochemistry, time itself takes on a different nature. It flies by and at the same time you seem to get lots done.

In Steve Taylor's excellent book called Making Time, he describes that time when you are in the airport lounge on the way home from holiday. You've read all your books and the plane is two hours late. Those two hours seem to last forever as all you do is twiddle your thumbs.

So when a project gets to its latter stages and you have less to do, it just seems that nothing is happening and progress has slowed to a crawl.

Secondly, by breaking a project down into prototype, alpha, beta and production versions, you don't get fooled into thinking you are 90% there when really you are only half way there.

Your crystallization here is to assign your own percentages to the build cycle - I've made some suggestions:

- Wireframe - 10%
- Alpha - 30%
- Beta - 30%
- Production - 30%

This way you never get fooled you are only 10% away from finishing.

Finally, the main reason why the last 10% seemingly takes so long is that conception and production, as for a baby, are just the first steps.

Once born, your light bulb moment assumes a life of its own, with the germination and production being just a small percentage of its lifespan.

## Flashbacks

Remember IKIWISI – I'll Know It When I See It.

Take small measured steps.

Test functionality and market sensitivity before you start production and then again as you go along.

Remember all feedback is useful and even if it sounds like criticism it is not to be taken personally. It's helpful to consider these views to avoid wasted time and effort on a idea that only seems great to you.

# 13

# The Chasm

*"The most dangerous thing in the world is to try to leap a chasm in two jumps."*
David Lloyd George

One of the biggest contributions to the initial excitement when you have a light bulb moment is the untold riches your new invention will bring.

People will love it; it will change the world; you can retire on the proceeds.

All these thoughts run through your head in less than a second, milling around with the thoughts connected with the inspiration itself. No small wonder that as your body is filled with such a cocktail of hormones that sanity can temporarily leave the room.

When your invention is grounded and the idea reaches production, a new reality sets in - you have to find people who want to make it, sell it, buy it and use it.

The marketing and sales effort has to kick in. If you are a 'solopreneur' - a one person band - that means it's all down to you. Often this can be a source of dismay for someone who loves the creative process and, all too often, things can grind to a halt.

Having a brilliant idea is great, but actually bringing the light bulb moment into physical reality is still only a small fraction of the process.

The most well known model for product and service life cycle is shown below and it is particularly relevant for new technologies. It follows a bell curve derived from the Gaussian curve after the German mathematician Carl Friedrich Gauss.

This curve also describes many other systems like quantum probability, genetic inheritance and even spread betting.

There is just one anomaly in this version known as The Chasm.

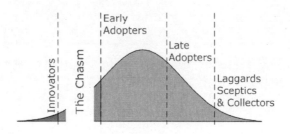

The Chasm describes the gap or hole that an idea might fall into that prevents it from gaining mass market appeal. The way to cross it is to take the light bulb moment and re-apply it continually over the product life cycle.

Of course, Edison was a master at this. He faced many chasms in his career but he never gave up, even to his dying day. He realized that the invention itself wasn't enough to ensure success. The systems around it were just as important and he was as tenacious as they come.

Take the electric light bulb. To make it work, you also needed an electrical generator, wires to carry the current and a light switch to turn the light on and off. Edison and his team designed and built each of these themselves from the ground up. Topsy, the elephant, played an unwitting part later in the development process.

His moment of real genius though wasn't the bulb or even the switch but the Edison screw which is still in use today. This allowed the bulb to be installed and removed without any technical knowledge or any danger if the current was still switched on.

Later innovators came up with the bayonet fixing and, even later still, a bulb that consumes less energy and doesn't need changing for years.

So as you can see, in the case of the light bulb, the product cycle is already over 100 years old and is likely to last for several hundred more, if we don't warm the planet up too much by using them.

For example, I am sure a hybrid bioluminescent and nano technology will be introduced in this century to create a myriad of innovative lighting solutions. Ironically, our science gets better when it more closely emulates natural processes that have been in existence for eons.

We would all be very proud if one of our light bulb moments was still in use long after we left this mortal coil. Here's how to apply light bulb moments to achieving that goal.

Over the product's life cycle, different types of users get involved with it.

## Innovators

In the first phase you find the Innovators. These are people who love being prime movers and getting into the latest and greatest 'thing'. They don't mind paying a small premium for a product and can be quite forgiving if a product has a few rough edges, even after beta testing.

They are often light bulb generators in their own right. They can take your product and use it to their advantage in ways that you hadn't envisioned. These are people you want on your side as it is by their application and reviews that you move your invention to the next stage.

The light bulb moment you can apply here is to initiate viral marketing campaigns so the Innovators become your unpaid sales team. By marketing their own first mover applications, they get as much, if not more, exposure as do you. It's a win-win situation.

## Early Adopters

Once the Innovators have paved the way, the Early Adopters are next in line for your amazing new invention. They are incentivised primarily by wanting to get on to a bandwagon. They are slightly risk averse, however, so they wait to hear how someone else gets on with it first - namely the Innovators.

They are driven by aspiration which is of course a linguistic variant of inspiration. Its etymology implies "to breathe upon" and "to be favourable to, to climb up to, to obtain, to reach".

The light bulb moments to invoke here are how to get the Innovator community to feed such aspirations of the Early Adopters.

A classic example would be when person A bought product B for price C and made more than C back in money as a result.

This neatly bypasses any price objection. The Early Adopter reasons they can buy it on a credit card and have the debt paid off before the bill is due.

Equally, it may be that the Innovator is simply having more fun, is healthier or more attractive as a result. You can't have enough case studies where you can demonstrate these benefits.

For example, I invented a widget in the 90's that allowed TV cameras to synchronize with computer screens to remove flicker. Once the producers cottoned on that this could be done, they wouldn't hire a TV crew unless they had one of my widgets with them.

The purchasers of my widget were more attractive to producers and, as a result, they got more business.

The proof of the benefits could be seen on many a TV program so I didn't need to advertise as I was indirectly already on the telly. My sales went up accordingly.

When the camera manufacturers installed the feature as standard a few years later, I was expecting all sales to fall off completely. At that point, it wasn't now a nice-to-have but an essential. Everyone with an old camera without this feature now had to either buy a new camera or buy my widget which was much cheaper.

I had unwittingly accessed the Late Adopter market and leapt over the Chasm.

What is probably most significant about this is was that I was at the time unfamiliar with this model and had no idea that anything like a chasm existed. As a young fearless 33 year old, the leap happened for me. If I was carrying the fear I may have just toppled in.

## Late Adopters

To get your product or service into the mass market, you have that small matter of the Chasm to cross. One way to deal with this is not to bother. Many companies use a bit of a sledge-hammer approach and just keep innovating niche products with the hope, and some knowledge, that one of them will leap the void into mass market acceptance.

There is nothing wrong with this as a tactic and it's a fun place to work. Innovators and Early Adopters will also pay a premium for a product so margins can be better too.

For example, modern day publishers are adopting this model as lower cost print on demand means you can speculate on more titles and authors.

If however global domination is your thing, there are two ways to cross the Chasm.

The first is to get someone to do it for you by selling your IP [intellectual property] and partnering with someone who has more global reach and buying power.

You can either sell out completely or negotiate a royalty deal for fewer margins but higher volume. This does mean also you can get on with the next invention.

The second way is to become that company with a global reach which has become much easier with the ubiquity of the Internet.

The Late Adopters are incentivized not so much by the innovation itself but by practicality. They want to know what it can do for them that they couldn't do before.

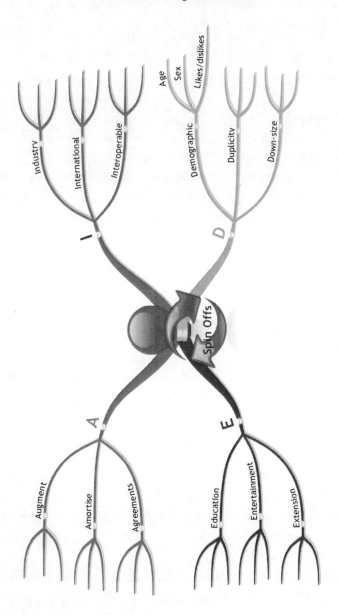

The light bulb moments needed here are twofold. To invent as many lateral applications for your invention as you can and then to find as many ways as you can to access the demographic groups who might be interested.

**Laggards and Sceptics**
I will group the last two types of customer into one classification as the approach to selling to them is similar. They are just interested in utility and price. They were the last to have a mobile phone and a broadband connection. Often they represent the older end of the population who might be somewhat set in their ways - or just have everything they need. Do not ignore this demographic as it is growing as an overall percentage of the population in the Western World and often has disposable income.

They will be motivated by necessity and low price. Either the old way of doing things is not available any more (like analogue TV) or it's actually becoming more costly not to adopt a new way of doing things.

The innovation required here is to find ways of making products cheaply in volume. For services, you might want to license or franchise them so more people can deliver your methodology. Again a bigger partner might be a useful ally.

**Collectors**
Somewhat ironically, at the end of a product's life cycle, it can sometimes acquire a rarity value and the Innovators start to buy them again at a premium.

In all these cases, the generation of light bulb moments in a marketing context will be made much easier by use of parallel thinking.

The IDEA acronym can be used in its original form - i.e. Inspiration, Dream, Evaluate, Actualise.

Alternatively, a more practical an approachable description might be something like this:

- Introduce
- Deliver
- Extrapolate
- Augment

Each time you extend your market reach, you approach a new sector, introduce your product and work out how best to deliver it.

The fun comes though when you extrapolate how your light bulb moment can be applied and augment the original idea - sometimes in a direction you did not foresee - the Spin Off.

## Crystallization 13: Generating Spin Offs

The best thing about spin offs is that they are like having a double light bulb moment. They augment and improve on your original idea. Even better still is that often it's not you but your Innovators or Early/Late Adopters that come up with them.

You can of course stimulate this process by running focus groups with customers or by interacting with them in online forums.

By far the best way, however, is to use our in built 'random association computer' - i.e. our brain - stimulated of course by the best association generator, a Mind Map.

I've also used as a seed the acronym IDEA and made up yet more things it can stand for.

Feel free to change these seed words to your own and add more. The task in this crystallization is, either by yourself or in a group, to think of as many ways as you can that your product or service could have spin offs.

To give you some guidance, what I mean by these labels is as follows:

- Industry - could it be applied in new sectors?
- International - could you change it so it works in new markets?
- Inter-operable - could it be made to work with more 'things'?
- Demographic - can it be sold to a new target market?
- Duplicity - can you replicate its essence, say with a minor change, but in such a way that it becomes something entirely new?

- Down-size - can it be made smaller, cheaper or with a subset of features?
- Education - how can it be made so that it can used to teach or be taught?
- Entertainment - how can you make it more fun?
- Extension - how can you make it bigger or add more features so it does something entirely new?
- Augment - how can you make it bigger or add more features so it's better value for money?
- Amortise - how can you spread the cost of production to improve cash flow or spread the cost of purchase to increase sales?
- Agreements - who could you partner with to get to new markets or so that 1+1 > 2 ?

This last point is crucial. At a certain point in your light bulb moment's journey, you will no longer be able to go it alone. To capitalize on all the spin off potential, you will need to bring in people to help you. The team you assemble is vitally important and can make or break your dream.

### Flashbacks

You can work to a model that never crosses the Chasm.
To cross the Chasm, you will need help or luck.
Be prepared to change your strategy over the product or service life time.
Capitalize on your asset through the Spin Off.

## 14

# The Wisdom of Crowds

*"There is no i in team"*
Anon

Taking a light bulb moments, making it happen in physical reality and crossing that chasm is rarely a solo effort.

In fact, the very nature of the entrepreneur and inventor is sometimes not best suited to product and service development, delivery and support.

Once the thrill of seeing the prototype come off the production line, apart from occasional promotional events - if they are not too shy - the inventor is classically back in research mode, working on the next, latest and greatest idea, often before the current idea has been fully brought to fruition - or even finished.

There is nothing wrong with that; the best teams are the ones where each member is playing to their strengths. That talent too should be recognized, cherished and nurtured.

Working out who is good at what is something all businesses should do - ideally as part of the recruitment process and then continually through staff management processes.

To help with this, there are many profiling systems in existence such as Myers Briggs. This was based on the Jungian system of archetypes (which in turn is based on the Major Arcana of the Tarot – something most corporate Human Resources teams probably won't know when they are planning the next staff development course). The Tarot itself is based on earlier systems like the I CHING.

The reason to make this comparison is that by going back to the root of the system it puts things in context.

The essential Jungian classification is between the rational and judging functions of thinking and feeling, and the so-called irrational, perceiving functions, such as sensing and intuition.

Myers Briggs extended this into eight classifications of personality types in the workplace: Extraversion, Sensing, Thinking, Judgment, and Introversion, iNtuition, Feeling, and Perception, which can be used in 16 different permutations.

Another way to look at these classifications is by looking back at the archetypes in the original source from which they were derived, the Major Arcana of the Tarot. This is comprised of 22 cards and these cards can be arranged in three rows of seven cards, for conscious, unconscious and higher self types of thoughts. These map neatly into the flavors and colors of thought. The one spare card is called the Fool, and The Fool is the wild card – the metaphor of its no-thinking innocence and brilliance representing the purity of the light bulb moment.

So what these profiling systems really show is where the mind of the individual primarily resides.

For example, the inventor and recipient of light bulb moments is tuned into their higher self, even if they aren't aware it even exists or even if they wouldn't especially want to acknowledge that it might exist.

The quality assurance manager who has amazing attention to detail will be working with most of their thoughts in the conscious mind - rooted to the physical plane. Both types have their place and both types are essential if the light bulb moment is to materialize.

When you then look at the Cascade of Creativity, it becomes clear that you either need one individual who is capable of switching their mind set from the etheric to the practical - or you need a team.

To do this, you can utilize the Mind Mapping processes, and ideally the breathing exercises, from Part 1 of this book in a group setting.

Ideally the team will also be aware of which mode of operation they are in - both collectively and individually, or they will be made aware of this using parallel thinking. The team must also be well aware of everyone's role and responsibility.

There is an excellent book by Mike Southon called the Beermat Entrepreneur. In it he describes how a company can grow from an acorn to a mighty oak, yet retaining that spark and entrepreneurial spirit of the early, heady years.

He advocates that each team should be a silo with an entrepreneur and four cornerstones. As the business grows, you then replicate this model much as Richard Branson did with the Virgin Group. This allows the team to retain its dynamism and ability to react quickly to changing market conditions.

Having four cornerstones around the progenitor of the light bulb moment gives a stable platform, much like a table with four legs. It also means the entrepreneurial inventor can be kept doing what they do best.

When you assemble your team, you can either use a profiling system or your gut mind. The latter is probably slightly more accurate. Irrespective of your approach, you need to prepare a specification for exactly what you want that each team member to deliver.

The mix of cornerstones varies a little depending on business type but in general it will look something like:

- Marketing and sales
- Production and delivery
- Support and training
- Legal and financial

In these days where we are globally connected, these teams can even be virtual and might never meet in person. I've delivered several iPhone applications this year working with a team like this that haven't met each other. One key team member and two clients I have never met face to face.

In this model, some cornerstones might not be needed on the project 100% of the time and they can operate in more than one team.

Each cornerstone can of course have staff working for them but the idea is that the entrepreneur can stay focused and not get involved with the minutiae of running the business.

Whole teams can also become cornerstones to other teams - for example, outsourcing companies that provide financial support.

I am sure you will recognize businesses that could benefit from such a simple and replicable model.

Accordingly using profiling systems up front is really useful when putting these teams together - as is management of ego as we will explore in the next chapter.

A key factor for success is for everyone to know and understand each other's role. A great way of doing this is to take a day out each month where everyone tries to do each other's job for a day. I used to do this on training days when I worked in the BBC on television production. Not only did it increase the bonding of the team but everyone learns new skills and comes to appreciate the work that their colleagues juggle, having 'walked a mile in their shoes'. Note that this can be done in business simulation and role playing games too.

The key skill that everyone should embrace is the use of the light bulb moment at all stages of product or service development and delivery. The generation of ideas should not be restricted to the central entrepreneur.

When a new product or service is brought to market, just getting it developed and ready for sale is often a mammoth task. And often the inspirational aspect of the business gets used just at the inception phase.

Perhaps the delivery was a little behind schedule, or resources a little thin on the ground as they are focused on keeping current clients happy. As a result, when the new product arrives it gets marketed, sold and delivered in the same way as its predecessor.

As a result of not really applying new thought to the new product, it might not take off as expected - perhaps hitting the technology chasm as described earlier.

The solution is to generate light bulb moments at all stages of production and delivery.

This means switching thought patterns and attention. The etheric thinker must become more grounded and the detailed person should be allowed to do some blue sky thinking and make suggestions too.

## Crystallization 14: IDEA about ideas

To do this, the first step is to document your current process for bringing a product or service to market. Say for example, it follows the route:

- Light bulb moment
- Market research
- Alpha prototype for internal appraisal
- Beta prototype for user testing
- Final production version
- Marketing
- User training
- Support

Take some time now to map your process. If using a Mind Map, use as large a piece of paper as you can find - at least A3 or tabloid. Draw the branches out as if the process was a clock face - start top left and go clockwise. Leave space for one or two levels of sub branches.

You then apply the IDEA process to each step, for example:

- Inspiration - brainstorm ideas for new ways of operating

- Dream - imagine how this would effect change
- Evaluate - test if it works
- Actualize - implement the change

This means you add at least four branches to each step. If you do run out of space on the page, you can draw an individual Mind Map for each stage of the process.

You can and should involve as many stakeholders as relevant and practically possible in this process.

As a result, you may find a new opportunity that was previously hidden to you. This process doesn't have to take a long time. It can be a great way to wind down on a Friday afternoon followed by a celebration that a light bulb moment has been crystallized.

Pausing for breath like this in a project sounds like it will add just a few extra days to its length but it can pay untold dividends.

The main benefit of this approach however is fostering the idea that everyone involved with product delivery is and should be capable of having a light bulb moment. It is not just the initial idea for the product that is important. A business nowadays has to innovate at all levels if it is to survive and prosper.

The resulting change in culture for a business is one where everyone's input is valued. This can only improve staff retention and profitability.

**Flashbacks**

The entrepreneur should be supported by cornerstones to bring the project to fruition.

The team approach allows retention of the creative spark.

The generation of ideas should not be restricted to the central entrepreneur.

Light bulb moments should be applied at all stages of production.

Celebrate your milestones as a team.

15

# Managing Ego

*"I think one of the interesting things about poker is that once you let your ego in, you're done for."*
Al Alvarez

No one person's ego can be allowed to dominate. Managing this at an individual and group level is vital.

Like many words in the English language, the meaning of ego has been modulated by usage and 'abusage' so that it now often carries a negative connotation.

We often hear something like, "He's got an ego the size of a planet."

Most commonly, but not exclusively, the word ego is used with reference to the male of the species.

The word ego is taken directly from Latin and is translated as "I myself". It was most popularised by Sigmund Freud who would have used the German term "Das Ich", which literally means "the I".

The ego is not intrinsically a bad thing. It just becomes so when it grows out of proportion and is then directed and used for its owner's aggrandisement.

A normal, healthy ego is what makes us self-aware and keeps us from self-harming. As we realize that other people are people too, with their own self awareness, our ego prevents us from harming those other people. Our words and deeds can indeed harm another as much as if our ego physically struck theirs. In some cases this can sometimes be more damaging and long lived.

Even though you can be on the wrong end of an inflated ego, much like our thoughts, you can't touch one or see one under a microscope or a brain image scanner. What can be detected however is areas of the brain that suffer damage that lead to a detachment which in turn leads to a disregard for one's self or for others. This can be seen in stroke victims who dispossess parts of their body and can, for example, put their hand in a flame because they think it doesn't belong to them.

The ego emerges around the age of seven and, like any aspect of ourselves, it needs nurturing and care. A healthy ego is mindful of others and is aware that by hurting or harming others, you are potentially damaging yourself.

The converse is also true. If you look after your ego by controlling the direction and the nature of your thoughts, it is amazing how those around you mirror what you are thinking. This gives an organization a choice to invoke a culture of fear and bullying or creativity, love and care. I know which one I would prefer to work for.

Sometimes though it can be difficult to change direction while you are still moving. The answer is to pause for a moment for a thought.

So, remembering that we are only programmed to be able to have one thought at a time (currently), if you think about a normal day at the office, think about how much time is devoted to ideas generation.

The diagram below is a massive generalization but I am guessing it is typical for many people.

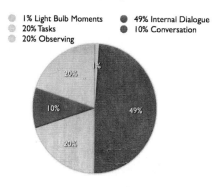

1% Light Bulb Moments    49% Internal Dialogue
20% Tasks    10% Conversation
20% Observing

When we are alone, driving to work or in a reverie, our thoughts often revert to our internal dialog. It will of course vary from day to day or from job to job but for many of us this takes at least half of our 'brain space'.

This dialog might be harbouring feelings of revenge, fear, anger or sadness. This can ultimately lead to a feeling of guilt for being silly enough to have been bothered about something that in retrospect was trivial. Alternatively, you might be daydreaming of what's happening at the weekend or thinking about unrequited love of a work colleague. These types of thoughts when shared as gossip around the water cooler or over email can lead to reduced morale. They certainly aren't focused on the work task in hand.

When we do spend time focusing on our work, this may involve a degree of observation such as reading, watching or listening. When any of these are done intently, our inner dialog is suppressed but it can cut in and out at any time.

We also spend time talking. When we are doing this, at least on the out breath, our inner dialog is temporarily halted.

At any time you can be interrupted by a colleague, a phone call or an email. It will then take you about five minutes to refocus on the task in hand. If the interruption annoyed you, it can ruin the rest of your day and stop all productivity and creativity stone dead.

With all this going on, it's not surprising for thoughts that could be light bulb moments to be so rare. They simply can't get a look in as the ego is working on all these other things.

To have more space for light bulb moments, it's not a case of suppressing the ego but more that it can benefit from being directed.

You can think of our thoughts having a psychic energy but not necessarily in a telepathic sense. Again by popular usage, the word psychic has come to refer to someone with extrasensory powers. The real definition means merely that something is influenced by the human mind or psyche. Just by switching from that glass half empty to glass half full perspective is enough to refocus and redirect your psyche.

So it's more that the energy we direct from our psyche directly leads to real world outcomes.

This is why the parallel thinking methodologies discussed earlier like de Bono's Six Thinking Hats are brilliant for controlling the focus of ego, especially in a group environment. The 'hats' used early on in the process allow all the negatives and fears to be tabled. By suppressing and marshalling the more controlling aspects of ego, this paves the way for the light bulb moments to appear. Many teams have a Devil's Advocate, who often delights in pouring cold water over any good idea, someone who is always an energy drain. With de Bono's Six Thinking Hats they get their chance early on to table their concerns and then be neutralized. Hopefully they might then even generate a brilliant idea.

What escapes many people is that we have full control over what we are thinking at any time. It's just that we have become accustomed not to think that we do, or even to think about it. In the same way that nobody can breathe for you or eat for you, nobody but you has control over your thoughts - unless you let them.

What is amazing about our thoughts is that just having a thought about them is enough to change them.

They are malleable, controllable and they also love to work to our best advantage. By far the best way to get them working with you is by taking up a meditative practice.

For many though their personal and business lives don't seem to allow this, it seems like a luxury of time. In which case, just a good walk is the next best thing. If this isn't possible, and in any case, I'd like to externally influence your thoughts with the diagram overleaf.

Imagine if you could be generating light bulb moments for a third of the time. You would then need to spend at least another

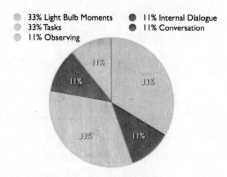

33% Light Bulb Moments    11% Internal Dialogue
33% Tasks    11% Conversation
11% Observing

third of the time focusing on tasks to bring them into physical reality. The remaining third can then be split amongst the 'normal' thought processes.

For some, just seeing this diagram might be enough to tip your thinking in a new direction. For others, I have designed this crystallization which not surprisingly came to me as a light bulb moment.

I spent no time worrying about it or chewing away at it. All I did was move to a task oriented mode of thinking by testing it on me and a few clients before writing about it.

When you get this level of trust in your own thoughts, what happens is that even better stuff starts to flow your way.

## Crystallization 15: Changing your mind

As I mentioned, we go about our days assuming our thoughts are random and also assuming that they are completely modified by external influences. It's not our fault the council is incompetent about picking up our waste or the government is managing the economy so badly. Someone else is obviously at fault as these events are out of our control.

Let me dispossess you of that notion. The other six billion and more people on the planet are probably spending their thinking time with similar thoughts. They are not out to get you or me. They haven't given it a moment's thought.

What's more, there are almost certainly a number of people on the planet who can benefit from your invention. Your task is just to make it affordable and accessible for them. If you were to switch your thinking from "woe is me" to "so how can I access this huge market", a different outcome will ensue.

And here's how to go about it:

Step 1: Sit in a chair with your back upright and imagine the top of your head is connected to the ceiling by a thin thread.

Step 2: Become aware of your breathing and consciously move your diaphragm - then close your eyes.

Step 3: Let the tension drop away from your body. Specifically we hold tension in our forehead, our neck, our jaw and our knees and ankles without being aware of it.

Step 4: Now become aware of your thoughts - let them mill around in your head for 30 seconds or so.

Step 5: Now start up a dialog with them.

You can ask them things like:

- where they came from
- who they belong to
- where they are going
- and who sent them

These are crazy questions, I know, but they are enough to get them under your control. After a while, your inner dialog gets fed up at being interrogated and gives up 'thinking'.

Step 6: You can then tackle specific types of thoughts with more direct questions and commands, such as:

Worries: Ask the worry to go away and be replaced by a solution. Be open to the solution.

Anger: Ask your Heart Mind if it would look after these types of thought so that your mind can be clear.

Past memories: If something comes up from the past that keeps bugging you, ask the associated remembrance to be replaced by those that can teach you what it was you need to learn. Be open to learning from it.

Self confidence: If you are worried about your own abilities, ask for a small sign to come along that will demonstrate to you that you are liked, loved and cherished.

Step 7: When you've experienced a change in thinking, open your eyes slowly.

Step 8: When these types of thoughts now occur to you in your 'waking state', quickly remember this visualization and replace them with an alternative thought pattern.

It takes a little time, a little practice, and a fair amount of trust, but once you get the hang of this, your life will start to take an unexpected turn for the better.

You will also find that your head feels clearer and light bulb moments occur more naturally. Rather than a torrent of inspiration that might overload you, you'll get a nice manageable stream which just seems to come along just at the right time.

## Flashbacks

Ego is not a bad thing. It is useful for self respect. It just needs to be managed and directed.

Interruptions take 5 minutes – or even all day - to recover from.

You have complete control over what you are thinking.

As a result, you have complete control over how you are feeling.

# 16

# The Future's Bright

*"Like gravity, karma is so basic we often don't even notice it."*
Sakyong Mipham

Irrespective of your religious beliefs or your spiritual persuasion, the concept of karma is really useful.

Like the word 'ego', however, the concept of karma has been hijacked by some people for dogmatic and controlling purposes. It is also sometimes castigated by the secular cynics for being utter nonsense and no more than a fairy tale.

Some people see karma rather simplistically as some form of cosmic retribution and magisterial system, doling out fines for transgressors and rewarding the good.

In fact it is even simpler than that. All it really means is that our current situation is a result of the summation of our life experiences to date.

It is completely optional, in my view, whether you choose to extend that over lifetimes we may have had before this one - or for lives yet to come.

It is however a good bet to look after the planet for our children and maybe just in case we have to come back to it one day.

One way of looking at karma is that it is a system whereby we can evolve, grow and learn. Now I have no proof or desire to postulate whether the multi-life version of karma is real or not. What I have experienced is that thinking and acting *as if* it might be true, seems to have a beneficial effect on our current lifetime, right now.

For some people, throwing salt over their left shoulder brings them good luck. In any case, it stops them worrying about bad luck.

If embracing the concept of karma helps you get along and improve your lot, it would be churlish to ignore it. So long as the salt doesn't go in someone's eye, and there's a little left for the meal, there is no harm done.

When you see karma as a model and not as a dogma, it brings a new insight that helps with the creative process.

In the multi-life version of karma, the belief is that we go to a place after we die to review the life we just had. In that same place, we plan the life we are about to have in terms of the learnings we want to embrace. This place has many names  from simply Heaven to the Akashic Records Office. These are of course metaphors to help us understand something that, if it does exist, sits outside our current existence and comprehension.

From the perspective of successfully grounding our light bulb moments, it brings a fresh and useful perspective - if not admittedly a little left field.

As you go about the thrill and pleasure of experiencing light bulb moments, perhaps during the grounding of them you experience certain trials and tribulations.

It is worth noting patterns that occur or recur in any hurdles you come across. In the context of karma, one theory is that these barriers are the types of experience you karmically agreed to tackle in this lifetime.

Another theory would be that you have somehow created these hurdles by one action leading to another. The helpful aspect of either of these theories, is if it makes you think about the situation a little, this may help you to be open to finding a solution.

In the same way that your thought patterns influence the world and your attitude to it, your reaction to these challenges completely affects the outcome and can alter the many possible outcomes.

You might easily be dejected by any adversity - your glass is half empty - or you can be thankful for the experience they bring - a glass half full attitude.

For example, you could be just about to launch your product but the beta testers find a flaw. Imagine how much time that would save compared to a product recall. You and your business might never recover from the financial implications and the marketing embarrassment.

A good indicator that a challenge has a karmic component is when you hit the same barrier a few times. It's like you are being reminded you need to deal with something.

What's more, when you step up to embrace challenges you end up with a 'glass over-brimming' situation. By dealing with the one thing you've been avoiding, opportunity seems to flow and something else changes, you get into your own flow.

If you have ever played a sport like golf or darts, you sometimes know when the dart leaves your hand or the ball leaves your putter that it's going exactly where you intended. Oddly enough, the flavor of thought you experience when you're in such a 'zone' is exactly the same as when you have a light bulb moment. I would hazard a guess that you weren't thinking at that exact moment of what you were having for supper.

So when you shift your thought pattern so that the internal dialogue is reduced, you allow space to notice more serendipity appearing in your life. You could also envision that the connection with the 'future you' from the superconsciousness is allowed to strengthen.

Once you cross this mental tipping point, all the events that help you with marketing and promotion of your idea start to happen around you, seemingly without you doing anything.

You find the perfect cornerstones for your business. You even meet the perfect investor to help you leap the Chasm in one go. In fact, the Chasm disappears from your life path. It was only there anyway to give you the karmic experience of learning how to cross it.

You friends, colleagues and family will recognize a new version of you. People will want to work with you, be with you and share with you.

What's more, in this new paradigm, you become cherished for the role you play as the progenitor of light bulb moments, and your team has bundles of complimentary flashes of inspiration to make your idea fly even higher.

Another karmic challenge you may experience now is having too much opportunity and choice. This soon dissipates when you realize it was something else you had to learn.

The answer, of course, was in your head all the time or, more specifically, it was blocked by the internal dialog and flavors of its thoughts.

When all this happens to you, then you might be hit by a pang of guilt. This is just too easy - there has to be a catch. So guess what happens then? A catch appears to confirm your suspicions.

If and when this happens, all you need to do is to realize the catch was only there so that you could learn and evolve some more. You then get back more into your flow.

Does all this sound too trite and too easy? Well the investment in trying it out is minimal as it just involves a slight shift in mindset. There is no particular downside. You do not have to change or adopt a new belief set or sign up to any mystical cult.

All you have to do is see potential challenges as being good things to help you grow as a person as opposed to some insidious agent, aimed directly at your ego, with the specific purpose of grinding you down.

This is why the management of your ego is such a crucial stage in capitalizing on your light bulb moment. Until it is brought home to roost, it will just create mayhem for karmic purposes.

## Crystallization 16: Voiding Karma

You can of course ignore everything in this chapter. If you believe in reincarnation anyway, anything you don't quite achieve in this life, you can deal with in the future. Now I'm not banking on coming back again. Accordingly, my aim is to get as much out of this life time as possible.

Even if you do believe in a multi-life model, none of its sensible proponents adhere to this instance of 'you' coming back but that your soul essence carries the karmic bank balance. So there won't be another Tom Evans quite like this one. This is as good as it gets for me and for you - unless I choose to make it even better.

What you can do is to simply choose to 'a-void' your karmic challenges.

The opposite approach is to void karma. To start this process going, complete the Mind Map, starting top right and going anti-clockwise as follows:

Step 1: Top right, list what goals you would like to achieve within these timescales with no limitations.

Step 2: Top left, list what physical, practical & psychological blocks stop you achieving all you desire.

Step 3: This is a win-win process, bottom left list what habits you would like to break at the same time.

Step 4: Finally, bottom right, in clearing these blocks & old habits, list what possible learnings you think you will obtain.

Now this latter step is something you may not be fully aware of at this stage. If you were, then you would be able to see the future. It does however give you an indicator of the areas in your life where karma can be voided.

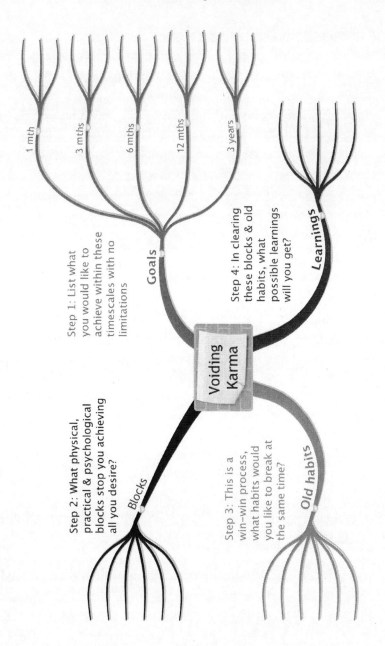

Once you start to void karmic challenges, you move to a whole new level of operation, you start to live magically.

## Flashbacks

Karma might seem a strange concept and have awkward connotations for you.

It is however another useful model to embrace.

Using it does not mean you have to change your belief set.

See it the bank account of your life and that you want to not only be in credit but for that credit to be increasing.

# 17

# Magic Moments

*"When magic becomes scientific fact, we refer to it as medicine or astronomy."*
Anton Lavey

Light bulb moments are pretty magical if you think about it. As if from nowhere, you get a gift of an idea when you least expect it. It's always much better than anything you could have come up with just by applying logic or reason. Additionally, they have that tendency to occur outside what we consider to be linear time - within a moment.

In Arthur C Clarke's book Profiles of the Future, he presciently stated, "Any sufficiently advanced technology is indistinguishable from magic."

Now some of what you have read so far might sound like it would be more at home in a grimoire - a magical text book.

I believe that this century is one when we will really start to fully understand the true power of our mind and the ability to manifest in physical reality from thought. So what we might think of as magical and mystical at the moment will come to be accepted by even the most dogmatic of materialistic scientists. At the same time, the religious and spiritual will find a framework which is less bound to blind faith and less susceptible to misinterpretation or even delusion.

Throughout this book you will have noticed my predilection for two things - alternate meaning of words and the use of a good acronym. This chapter is no exception.

To help summarize how to invoke this particular type of magical moment, I've coined another acronym of MAGIC:

- Meditation
- Association
- Generation
- Intention
- Collaboration

To make this type of magical spell work best, they need to be applied in a judicious manner both AT the right moment and WITH the right moment.

What I refer to here is the other non-temporal definition of the word moment, namely:

a) a tendency to produce motion, especially about an axis.
b) the product of a physical quantity and its directed distance from an axis.

By applying your MAGIC with the application of a relatively small amount of force and with the right lever, you can move a mountain.

Let me explain the five elements of the acronym.

**Meditation**

This starts with the breath and learning to enjoy the benefits of a quiet mind.

The tools to invoke in this process are noticing the flavor of your thoughts and then passing them to the appropriate vestigial minds to better process them. As a result, the inner dialogue abates and you are poised to tap into the superconsciousness.

The meditation too can take any form. A reflective walk in nature or listening to soothing music. Tai Chi or yoga is fine too. The aim is just to make that inner voice be quiet for a while each day.

## Association

Mind Maps are the tool of choice. You don't need to use any special software, paper and pencil is all you need. A stick in the sand could also be used. By free association, your whole mind is free to find connections that were obscured by the logical mind.

By using color, images and one word per branch, your mind will make better quality associations and you will better spot coincidences.

Mind Maps can contain semantics such as clockwise for forward time and anticlockwise for reflection and regression. Placing goals and the future top right and past events on the left may also be useful. Note that this doesn't apply for all people and especially those with dyslexic or autistic tendencies who might have different neural 'wiring'.

The key is for free flow, no rules, and for the mind to be allowed to wander. Just doing a drawing or doodle of what is on your mind and what comes to mind is often useful.

When you finish a Mind Map, stare at it with your eyes defocused for 30 to 60 seconds. Even though it is blurred, your brain and mind will absorb it and remember all its detail. It does this in a way such that the unconscious mind makes the conscious mind aware of anything connected with the Mind Map that's important as and when it appears.

## Generation

To realize your moment, you have to generate action. This means making a prototype, testing your idea and bringing it into reality and out of the superconsciousness before someone else does.

Remembering the other acronym IKIWISI - your colleagues and potential customers will only Know It When They See It when it ceases to be just in your mind's eye.

Small steps are important here. Any adversity, fear or resistance is simply a sign that there is something you need to deal with. See it as part of your karmic journey.

## Intention

This is something we haven't discussed explicitly before but it's the first step in magnifying your magical force by using 'mechanical moment'.

If you approach the application of your light bulb moment with the right intent, it has the effect of amplifying it. It is almost like you are dropping a bigger pebble of thought into the pool of superconsciousness. The ripples it creates get picked up by others who get drawn to you.

When setting the right intention, you might choose not to have riches as your prime goal but perhaps something more altruistic, even if it is your own personal development. In my experience, your required financial reward still comes along but in a way that you didn't necessarily expect.

What seems to carry the best moment is when your aim is to add value and augment the collective thought pool.

Make the 1 year and 3 year goals in the voiding karma crystallization big ones.

## Collaboration

This is the final piece of the magical jigsaw. By working in teams, you spread knowledge, leverage the wisdom of the crowd, and you trigger light bulb moments in others. In short, your magic spreads and infects others - in a nice way of course.

When you tackle growth collectively, you are also able to void karma at a group level. This is very powerful magic indeed. To void karma in groups, just repeat the crystallization from the last chapter collectively with your team.

When you take this approach, you become a real magician and an unstoppable force. Your light bulb moments start to crystallize in front of your eyes.

### Crystallization 17: The importance of ritual

In days gone by, performing even basic magic required the usage of elaborate rituals. These were often shrouded in secrecy and passed on verbally. If they were written down, often deliberate errors were introduced just in case they fell into the wrong hands.

Nowadays we have a deeper understanding and mastery of the physical world. We use devices every day like mobile phones without a second thought that would appear to be magical to someone who travelled forward in time from just a century ago. Just imagine being able to speak to anyone on the planet from a device that weighs a few hundred grams. They even have cameras nowadays so you can see people.

In anyone's book that's magic - unless of course you know how light gets converted into electrical signals and then digitized and compressed and multiplexed over the airwaves and down optical fibres.

In parallel with these amazing leaps forward in technology, magic is relegated to sleight of hand and other such chicanery. Note that even stage magicians perform small rituals to deflect your eyes and attention. There is no space for 'real' magic to happen in our modern day world.

Well that's only if you don't want it to or don't want to recognize it when it happens to you or for you. Now remember there could well be a rational explanation for these occurrences and for it only to appear to be magic as we don't fully understand it yet.

The magic referred to here is gentle stuff. We are not conjuring demons or sticking pins into voodoo dolls. This magic conjures up wondrous ideas in the form of light bulb moments followed by amazing happenstance that brings them into physical existence.

The modern day rituals to make these light bulb moments are actually pretty pragmatic and easy to carry out. The Illuminations and Crystallizations at the end of each of these chapters are all good examples - with any of the shamanic window dressings removed.

This crystallization can be applied in addition to any of the exercises. It's intrinsic to the way we operate as humans but it's often forgotten or overlooked in our busy world.

It's simply this.

Firstly, when you have a light bulb moment or a stroke our good luck, remember to say "Thank you". It doesn't matter if it's to another human being, your pet, your god or guardian angel, something inanimate like your desk. Just remember to give thanks.

Secondly, when you hit a milestone in the grounding of your light bulb moment, like a product launch, or a book signing, make sure you celebrate. How hard is that?

Lastly make sure you share your success story with others, perhaps as a press release, a blog or a case study.

The C of Celebration can also be the last C in the acronym of MAGIC. As for the IDEA acronym, feel free to make the MAGIC your own too by giving it your individual take for each letter. That way it works even more powerfully.

## Flashbacks

Magic exists; we just don't yet fully understand it or recognize it.

When we understand magic, it becomes known as science.

Science is, after all, the new alchemy.

Meditation is the first key.

Association makes the new connections.

Generation takes it from the ethereal to the physical worlds.

Intention amplifies it and gives it more moment.

Collaboration spreads and shares the magic.

Celebration seals the magic and allows the loop to continue.

## 18

# A Whole New Mind

*"The mind is like a parachute. It doesn't work if it's not open."*
Frank Zappa

There is a huge collateral benefit from learning to have light bulb moments on demand. By learning the arts of whole brain thinking and whole mind not-thinking, you begin to operate on a whole new level.

Things that used to annoy you become trivial. New connections appear in your life in the form of people, ideas and opportunities.

What's equally amazing is that this capability is open to all, it's free and nobody owns it as a philosophy or methodology. You can add to it, take bits from it, morph it, bend it, shape it and use it.

Indeed, I've only put this book together with the help of previous prior art from luminaries such as Newton, Edison and Jung. I have borrowed extensively from Walt Disney, Edward de Bono and the father of Mind Maps, Tony Buzan.

To make this journey, just like any other, you first have to recognize where you are starting from and have some idea of where you want to get to - and why. Remembering at all times the experience of the journey itself and not just arriving at the end destination is vitally important and enjoyable.

I stress that is not about creation of an elite or gaining power over others. This kind of magic only works when you adopt a high ethical position. It's crucial you keep ego well under control. In addition, everyone on the planet is on a different point and route down their karmic path.

I mention this as the three states of mind I am about to mention are all pretty amazing in their own right. None is better than the other and you can choose to work with any of them as best suits you and your situation. You also need to experience all of them to appreciate the others. I suspect also that there are many more states still and that they are accessed by cycling around these states in a spiral manner.

## The Dormant Mind

For many people, there is an assumption that the cards they have been dealt with are it. Their thoughts mirror those of others and the current collective mood of the nation. If the government and the press say we are in recession, then they believe it.

The world tends to happen around them and their lives are 'at effect'.

Does this sound terrible? Well no, the fact that a living being can even have thoughts and be self aware is nothing short of amazing. In this state, you can achieve incredible things. You can love, laugh and be in awe of nature or art. You can be entertained and you can entertain others. You can cry, be fearful or guilty, be hurt and be angry.

All in all, this is an amazing feat for something which is around 75% water, 20% carbon and the rest a mix of other atoms. This mind can also walk around largely unaided, feed itself and, in collaboration with others, fly itself to the Moon and back.

Dormant minds are not bad minds but they are easy to spot. They might chat incessantly about themselves, their football team or the weather. They might be unlucky in love or in life or fearful of both. They might have one of those egos that are the size of the planet. They might be serial entrepreneurs who have a string of ideas that never quite seem to make it off the drawing board.

They might have a sneaking suspicion that there must be more to life than this.

## The Awakening Mind

This state of mind occurs to those with Dormant Minds who wake up one day and decide that there must be more to life. This realization can also come in the form of a light bulb moment, much like Saint Paul on the road to Damascus. Indeed, many people who experience near-death experiences go through such a transformation.

Some people are born with an Awakened Mind but have to grow through some form of dormancy as they become self aware and indeed educated. These are the bright kids on the block who show extraordinary talent and perspicacity from a young age.

Those who awaken in their 30s and 40s tend to do it either as their children leave the nest or when they leave the assumed security of the corporate world.

Some awakening people become addicted to alternative therapies, visit sweat lodges or try and communicate with other dimensions. If they don't get an immediate result and then become disenchanted with their experience, they can end up back in a dormant state.

The route to an awakened mind is much simpler. It's to become aware of what is around you and to become awake to serendipity. It's equally important to appreciate both the natural world and 'human-made' achievements and not eschew one over the other.

The beauty of a sunset has equal status with the microprocessor that drives your mobile phone. They are formed from the interaction of the same stuff - matter, energy and consciousness. The beauty is literally in the eye of the beholder.

Those with awakened minds are collaborators and team players. They know that 1+1 equals at least 3.

They accept adversity as opportunity and, as a result, they become luckier. For example, their light bulb moment might come from recognizing adversity and realizing they have the wisdom and resources to do something about it.

They are not limited by the world around them as they have the power to shape it. They become truly alive and a force not only to be reckoned with but one you want to be around. They begin to live at cause.

## The Merged Mind
There is only a small step to take from an awakened mind into a merged mind. In some ways though, it's also like taking a step back several thousand years to when humankind was one with nature. Everything had a rhyme and a reason and nothing is separate from anything else.

As Chief Seattle said, "All things are connected. Man did not weave the web of life; he is merely a strand on it."

By the way, I lose count of the times quotes even as brilliant as this never mention women - I'm sure it's just a cultural thing but a habit that could do with some re-balance.

The merged mind is fully open to all possibilities. It treasures every moment and pays attention to every thought. It is as attentive to the external and the internal.

To a merged mind, adversity is seen not just as an opportunity but as a sign. It's a sign that no matter how far they have personally developed; there are still an infinite number of rungs on the evolutionary ladder and still much to learn. The adversity has merely been presented as the next learning.

The merged mind is open to a limitless stream of light bulb moments but equally aware of the need to ground them. They are also able to spot the good ones and ignore or even give away the ones that are not for them.

They are mind-full of the nature of their thoughts and have an amazing capacity to multi-task. The merged mind can run an inner dialogue and receive inputs from the superconsciousness simultaneously.

It acheives this because the conscious mind and Higher Self have become fused with and by the unconscious mind.

It is then capable of a re-found ability which could potentially transform our society.

If you think about it, we can normally only influence the outside world by the noises we make and the mechanical actions we take. So our voice can influence people by the words we say and a ballet dancer can amaze the audience with their grace and ability. We can also shout angrily at someone or type some words that offend.

The merged mind is able to output in three 'new' ways:

- influence just on a thought
- attraction via a thought
- healing from thoughts, often helped by words spoken or written

The healing capability is particularly effective on dis-ease brought on by an unbalanced state of mind.

What is happening neurologically is that the merged mind is starting to tap into the 90% or so of the brain that we haven't fully understood yet. Many children are now being born with merged minds and you may hear references to them as indigo and crystal children. They have amazing capabilities but, as children, they still need to mature and they need much love and support.

From a functional perspective, they are attuned to the super-consciousness and are relaxed with the knowledge that most thoughts aren't necessarily their own.

Those with merged minds are creators, catalysts and connectors. They are also meek, humble and thankful of their ability. They are reflective and don't take themselves too seriously. They seem to possess an unlimited capacity for adapt-ability, compassion and absorption. They heal both themselves and others upon a thought.

As I mentioned, they also choose to have periods of dormancy and re-awakening. They use natural time to achieve this, flowing with the day, the Moon and the seasons.

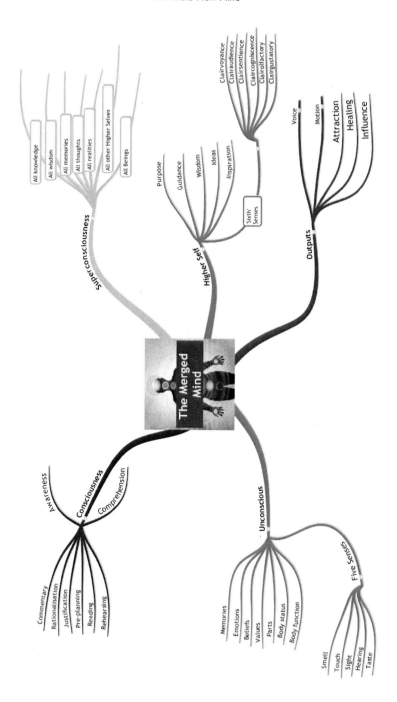

The Merged Mind

**Superconsciousness**
- All knowledge
- All wisdom
- All memories
- All thoughts
- All realities
- All other Higher Selves
- All Beings

**Higher Self**
- Purpose
- Guidance
- Wisdom
- Ideas
- Inspiration
- 'Sixth' Senses
  - Clairvoyance
  - Clairaudience
  - Clairsentience
  - Claircogniscence
  - Clairolfactory
  - Clairgustatory

**Outputs**
- Voice
- Motion
- Attraction
- Healing
- Influence

**Consciousness**
- Awareness
- Comprehension
- Commentary
- Rationalisation
- Justification
- Pre-planning
- Reading
- Rehearsing

**Unconscious**
- Memories
- Emotions
- Beliefs
- Values
- Parts
- Body status
- Body function
- Five Senses
  - Smell
  - Touch
  - Sight
  - Hearing
  - Taste

The essence of this state and any state of mind is simply this. We are all equipped with the ability to choose which thoughts we have and how to use them to map our way in this world.

We are all co-creators.

## Crystallization 18: Making your mind up

The most important learning from this chapter is that nobody but you has control over what you think or do.

There is no religion that is more right than any other and no system or methodology that you should or must follow.

If you like all of this book and fancy having a dabble with a merged mind, then give it a go. If you think that all of this book is drivel, then use it to prop up a wobbly table or give it to someone else. If you like just some bits of it, then use those bits only.

If you have just one light bulb moment as a result of reading it, then that is fine too.

The concepts in this book are so ethereal and intangible in nature, you cannot use your logical mind to decide if they are right or wrong and for you - or not.

Using the left brain alone will stop light bulb moments in their tracks. If you rely on your right brain alone, your inspirations will never see the light of day.

The proof of this particular pudding is in seeing your ideas manifest into the physical world. Taking the first step along the way involves a little trust.

Accordingly, this last crystallization is simple and intentionally brief.

You must use your gut and heart minds to guide you to answer these simple questions with a simple yes or no.

1. Is your mind dormant?
2. Is your mind awakened?
3. Is your mind merged?

Irrespective of your answer, you have three options you can take separately or jointly.

1. Ask your gut and heart what you would like to do next.
2. Go for walk, look up mostly, and let a light bulb moment come in.
3. When you next go to sleep, ask your unconscious mind to give you a dream that will give you the inner-sight you need.

If as a result you get a sign or a new thought comes in, act upon it as you may never know where it may lead.

## Flashbacks

There is nothing wrong with adopting any of these states of mind.

Dormant minds are capable of amazing things.

Awakening minds are aware that there is even more potential.

Merged minds start to experience some of that potential, yet know that there is so much more yet to come.

When you experience a light bulb moment, your mind is merged with all others momentarily.

**To your illumination with luv, luk & lux**

Tom Evans
Surrey Hills
June 2010

# Recommended Reading

Advanced Banter, John Lloyd and John Mitchinson, Faber & Faber, 2008

Beermat Entrepreneur, Mike Southon, Prentice Hall, 2002

BOOM, Emma Wimhurst, Diva Publishing, 2009

Edison: A Life of Invention, Paul Israel, John Wiley & Sons, 1998

Embracing the Wide Sky, Daniel Tammet, Hachette Livre, 2009

How to Mind Map, Tony Buzan - Thorsons, 2002

Isaac Newton: The Last Sorcerer, Michael White, Fourth Estate, 1998

Making Time, Stephen Taylor - Icon Books, 2007

Mind Mapping for Business, Tony Buzan and Chris Griffiths, BBC Active, 2010

Science and the Akashic Field, Ervin Lazlo - Inner Traditions, 2007

Six Thinking Hats, Edward de Bono, Penguin, 2000

The Dream Whisperer, Davina Mackail, Hay House, 2010

The Field, Lynne McTaggart - Harper Collins, 2003

The Holographic Universe, Michael Talbot - Harper Collins, 1996

The Master & His Emissary, Ian McGilchrist, Yale University Press, 2009

The Phenomenon of Man, Teilhard de Chardin - Perennial, 2002

The Physics of the Soul, Amit Goswami - Hampton Roads, 2001

The Self Aware Universe, Amit Goswami - Tarcher Putnam, 1995

The Wizard of Menlo Park, Randall Stross, Three Rivers Press, 2007

Time, Alexander Waugh, Headline, 2000

Unleash the Idea Virus, Seth Godin, Simon & Schuster, 2000

Waking From Sleep, Steve Taylor, Hay House, 2010

Wizard: The Life and Times of a Genius: Nikola Tesla, Marc J. Seifer, Kensington Publishing, 1996

# Resources

The Mind Maps used in the book are available as a free download from: www.tomevans.co.

Just use the the acronym introduced in chapter 17 of this book as a discount code on checkout to get them for free.

Note that they are in the .imm format for Tony Buzan's iMindmap software which is available for a free 7 day trial at www.thinkbuzan.com

iMindmap works on Windows and Macintosh and is also available for the iPhone and iPad.

With these templates and this software, 7 days is more than enough time to have any number of light bulb moments. I guarantee though that you will find the software really useful in all areas of your personal and business lives.

There are also a set of MP3 audio visualizations to accompany this book that take you to heightened states of consciousness, such as:

- The Quantum Collapse of Thought: how to still your inner voice
- Re-minding Yourself: connecting with your vestigial minds
- Alpha Awakening: connecting with the superconsciousness
- Journey to the Akashic Records: discovering your karmic path
- Embedding Mind Maps in your Neurology: how to spot serendipity
- The Inspirational Breath: how to get in 'the zone'

The event calendar for the Art and Science of Light Bulb Moments workshops and talks is also on the website.

# About the Author

Tom Evans is 21st century Renaissance man. He has been described as being something between a polymath and a jack of all trades and master of none.

Throughout his career he has been a serial entrepreneur always working at the leading edge of technology. He has been living and breathing Light Bulb Moments since he was a child.

When not writing his own books, he mentors other authors and creatives on how to banish writer's block and tap into their Creative Muse. He also acts as a catalyst, visionary and a seer [see-er] for businesses looking for new ideas and strategies.

As a boy, he was fascinated by the magic of TV and radio and used to take them apart to find out how they worked. Sometimes, to his parents' chagrin, he had a few bits left over.

After taking a degree in Electronics, he embarked on a career as a broadcast engineer with the BBC. By the time he was 25, he was working with Sony Broadcast and recognized as one of Europe's leading experts on camera and imaging technology.

By the time he was 30, he had his own company manufacturing innovative widgets to broadcasters worldwide. He'd also received two Royal Television Society awards for his inventions and had several patents to his name.

In the 1990's, when the Internet came along, Tom built a new business providing innovative ecommerce and epublishing solutions for dot.com startups and established corporates.

Like many authors, he ended up being one sort of by accident.

Like many people in his mid-forties, he paused for breath, took a holiday after giving up a perfectly good job without another one to go to. On holiday, he wrote some poetry, made it into an ebook and to his surprise people started downloading it - and paying for it. He had become an unexpected author.

A year later, the 100 Years of Ermintrude became a trilogy of interlocking stories and ended up in print. Somewhere along the way the downloads also raised loads of money for Walk the Walk breast cancer charity and Tom ended up walking round London in a bra for 26 miles. Now that same book has just been published as an iPhone app. As an irrepressible technophile, Tom has also developed many iPhone and iPad applications.

The process of writing of this book by accident fascinated Tom and he started to research the true nature of thought, where ideas actually come from and what stops them in their tracks.

He has become a student of both the esoteric and exoteric and switched his personal research direction from technology to the magic of the human mind.

He has now trained as a hypnotherapist and specializes in past life regression and future life progression techniques. He is able to see all possible futures and helps clients manifest the ideal one for them.

He is also a Master Trainer for Tony Buzan's Mind Mapping software and teaches both Whole Brain and Whole Mind Thinking.

He started working with other authors on a one-to-one basis three years ago and he has helped many authors get in print. He has also delivered many creative writing and ideas generation workshops.

His second book, simply called Blocks, shows the enlightened way to clear writer's block and how to connect with unlimited creativity. Removing blocks of course is a natural precursor to having unlimited light bulb moments on demand.

Since writing this book, Tom has just written a companion book called Flavours of Thought: Recipes for Fresh Thinking which expands on the ideas in chapter 9 of this book. It is available both in print and the Kindle Reader.